Southern Accents on
COLOR

Southern Accents on
COLOR

FRANCES MACDOUGALL

WITH THE EDITORS OF

Southern Accents

Bulfinch Press   AOL Time Warner Book Group   Boston New York London

Contents

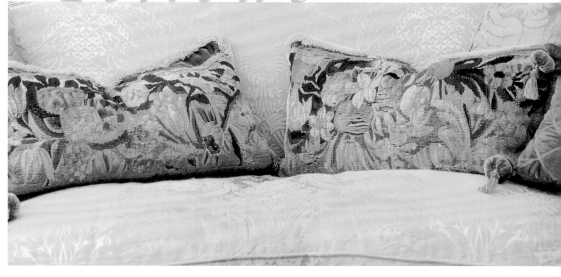

Thanks are due to all my colleagues at *Southern Accents,* who make work a delight and constant source of colorful experience. I'd especially like to thank our editor, Karen Carroll, a great friend and source of support, inspiration, and guidance for more years than I'll mention here. I owe my friend executive editor Lindsay Bierman sincere gratitude because of his thoughtful ear and creative insight, and for producing the images for the magazine that appear in this book. Our photography coordinator, Karen Downs, has been a wonder at tracking film. Over the last year we've had several interns, including Rebecca Beach, Mary Architzel, Jennifer Maxwell, Margaret Whiteside, and Clare Martin, whose help has been invaluable. I'd like to thank our contacts at AOL Time Warner Book Group: publisher Jill Cohen; associate publisher Karen Murgolo; Dorothy Williams, who has edited our books with discrimination and perspicacity since 1997; and Jean Wilcox, whose design brings the photos to life. And of course Thierry, Ellie, and the little one on the way.

First edition

Library of Congress Cataloging-in-Publication Data

MacDougall, Frances.

Southern Accents on color / Frances MacDougall, with the editors of Southern Accents. — 1st ed.

p. cm.

ISBN 0-8212-2811-0

1. Color in interior decoration — Southern states. I. Southern Accents. II. Title.

NK2115.5.C6.M33 2003

747'.94 — dc21   2002027954

Bulfinch Press is a division of AOL Time Warner Book Group.

Designed by Wilcox Design

PRINTED IN SINGAPORE

Introduction

Color is so elemental, so integral to our everyday existence, that we can't help but take it for granted. If we stopped and marveled at every new shade, new tone, new expression of hue, the world would stop. The sheer vastness of the spectrum is overwhelming. Color is a fundamental notion that we grasp at the earliest age. Newborns see in black and white, but as their perceptions of color evolve, so do they. Pediatricians advise decorating infants' rooms in primary colors because they stimulate brain activity. Children — even as young as two years old — can identify a favorite color earlier than they determine a favorite food.

This passion for color continues through life. The colors of food help us determine our preferences. If I purchase an article of clothing, the first criteria is the color. An unflattering color, and it's not even worth trying on. If for the past twenty years there has been a death of color, now, at the beginning of the twenty-first century, much can be made of its vibrant return. At its height, the fashion for no-color colors meant that form was the most important element in a room. Whites and beiges took on a subtle or serene role next to collections, furniture, and art. But times and tastes have changed.

Is an increased desire to connect with nature as we become more techno-savvy and more disconnected from our natural environment at the turn of the millennium what makes us seek out color now? Or is it just about time? New Orleans decorator and antiques dealer Patrick Dunne says, "All art is a function of confidence — reflective of society and of oneself. The ripening of any civilization or culture is evidenced in the use of the richness of color."

In the South, where the climate and the landscape collaborate on colors with an intensity so profound they seem manufactured rather than natural, colorful interiors have never gone away. Even the neutral rooms that appear in *Southern Accents* are always shot with a shade that makes everything else in the room look more interesting, more personal.

Color is personal. As much as I try to live with other colors, green seems to be the shade I return to again and again. All of the public rooms in my house — the entry, the living room, the dining room — are sage or a variation of it. I don't even wear that much green, so I cannot explain it. Some might say it has to do with my Southern upbringing, where landscape and light are as important as graciousness and heritage. My mother chalks it up to all the celadon porcelain that surrounded me in my formative years. My parents met and married in the 1960s in Cambodia and brought back exquisite celadon vases that I remember admiring even as a young child. Whatever the reasons, color is such an important part of my world and the world we cover at *Southern Accents* that there is no end to the inspiration we find in its varieties.

There are reasons as complex as a color's components to explain what makes one person seek out blue over green, yellow over gold, brown over gray. History, even fashion, plays a part, as do our own personal histories. In this country, in the 1930s, we sought out Williamsburg or colonial revival colors, those shades that we thought derived from our colonial forebears — pale blues, soft yellows, muted greens. Fast for-

Green is such an integral part of the Southern psyche, four different designers created headboards in that color when we produced a story on the subject. Paul Garzotto's included a diaphonous silk embroidered with butterflies on a Venetian shape.

ward to the last decade, when Colonial Williamsburg totally revamped its color palette as a result of intensive research. Thorough paint analysis, which involved scientifically scraping away layers of color and paper, helped curators discover that those shades we thought were so subtle were actually fuchsia, kelly green, royal blue. The newly re-painted, repapered rooms at the historic site almost shock with their intensity. Curators recognized that many early colonial colors had faded and lost their muscle over the centuries; in truth, the anemic colors we attributed to our Puritan ancestors were originally much more passionate than previously thought. Of course, we can also blame a desire for status on our ancestors. Paint was expensive, as were fabric and upholstery, so a colorful home suggested a prolific provider.

The colors we choose to live with today are not, fortunately, just those shades that were used in this country two hundred years ago. Dunne says, "Color has to relate to the environment — geographical as well as cultural." Designers are inspired by colors from around the world: the deep green of Balinese terraced rice paddies, the airy ice blue of Swedish grand manors, the gold in ancient Egyptian tombs, the pink of Palm Beach bougainvillea — the list is too long to even consider completing. In the eighteenth century, when the ancient cities of Pompeii and Herculaneum were discovered, an entire decorative movement, known as Neoclassicism, began. It endures to this day. Not only were styles and decorations influenced, but also the faded once intense colors of frescoes inspired a palette that affected all of Europe.

The colors that paint our subconscious are as interesting as souvenirs brought back from foreign travel. For years, I've associated the colors of France with the small-scale patterns and blue and yellow shades of sunny Provence. It wasn't until I met my French husband and visited his family home in Brittany that I learned of the royal, maritime blues and the lush pinks of the *hortensia* in the area. The rich colors of Brittany brighten a region grayed by perennial mist that blocks out the sun but hydrates the greenery. Color around the world is a reflection of an area's history, its environment, and its personality.

And of course colors are subject to the evolution of trends. Fashion magazines' headlines may herald "Orange Is the New Beige" or "Black Is Back," one season to the next. Diana Vreeland, legendary editor of *Vogue* and *Harper's Bazaar,* proclaimed that pink was the navy blue of India, and legions of followers rushed to add a dash of it to their wardrobes, if not their homes. Our interiors are no different. If we aren't wearing hunter green, we certainly don't want to live with it in our homes. You may debate who influenced whom, the fashion or the home decoration industry. Either way, there are definitely shades that are "in" and shades that are "out." But fashions are fleeting; hopefully our interiors are not. Trends come and go. Colors may be hot or not, but every color has an application that goes beyond what is au courant. Our industry has evolved around color forecasting, but on close inspection one realizes that generally the same colors are pronounced "in" season after season. They are often given sexy or interesting new labels or names to heighten their appeal. For example, chartreuse was the new color a few years ago. Now it's apple green.

"People see something they like, and then another person sees it, likes it, and then uses it," says Birmingham architect Bill Ingram. "Before you know it, everybody is using that color, and it becomes tired." The trick with colors is to select a shade or a tone that will not become tired. Atlanta designer Jackye Lanham says, "You know I love teal, and I work it into many of the interiors I do. But we can't call the color 'teal.' It puts people off. But I haven't had anyone complain when we find another term" — blue green, sea green, to name just a couple. Ultimately, trends are relative. "You can say this color is out or that color is out, but if a room is beautiful, it's beautiful. There's no way around it," says Lanham.

In these pages we will visit the houses that have appeared in *Southern Accents.* We will look at the variety within specific colors. We will also get perspectives from the designers whose work appears in the magazine. For as personal as color choices are, they can be extremely challenging to translate into an interior. Sure, I love green, but determining an affection for a color is a long way from selecting variations that will

OPPOSITE: Blue cushions stuffed for comfort give substance to the black lacquer cane chairs. The blue brings a shot of brightness to the otherwise monochromatic space, and draws the color out of the abstract painting hanging above.

In this Houston apartment, luminescent mocha-shaded velvet covers the sofa and club chairs. The 1940s mirrored chest reflects black and white, and black in the art, lamp shades, and coffee table give the room definition.

work together to create compelling contrasts. Color should feel so right that it's almost not even noticed. You just recognize the wholeness of the room.

Living with color does not mean simply painting the walls red or green. Carefully orchestrated colors in the hands of a skilled designer can speak volumes to you and about you, and it's knowing how to manage the two that makes things interesting. Matisse said, "It is not enough to place colors, however beautiful, one beside the other; colors must also react on one another. Otherwise, you have cacophony."

And while the magazine has always sought out great Southern interiors, which happen to reflect a love of color, other areas of the country are catching on. Even as a more modern aesthetic is being embraced — spare spaces, clean lines — color in the form of pretty pastels and bold accents has definitely taken root as well.

On Rooms and Colors

Blue: We see it most often in coastal settings. Blue shows up in bedrooms and nurseries (not just for a boy anymore) and as pale color in living rooms.

Yellow: One of the most versatile colors, yellow creates the illusion of light in rooms with few windows, but it will also look great in a light-filled room where natural light will make it appear paler. We see it most often in kitchens, bathrooms, bedrooms, and dining rooms.

Green: When you're looking for a neutral color but still want color, green is a great choice. It's always present outside and can be toned down inside, especially in living rooms, family rooms, and garden rooms.

Red: It's a stimulating color, so red is a great and obvious choice in a dining room. It's a bold backdrop that begs for equally strong accessories — like great silver and porcelain.

Purple: It's hard to take too seriously in anything other than a bedroom, where it strikes the perfect balance between pretty and pale.

Pink: In varying degrees of intensity, it may show up in living rooms and master bedrooms as well as a little girl's room. As an accessory, in rugs, pillows, ceramics, and art, a little pink goes a long way toward softening hard edges and bringing in pretty color.

White: It makes other colors stand out, so it's a great accent color. White also shows up in modernist spaces and serene bedrooms.

Brown: Use it where you want to create a cocoon, like a bedroom or a small living room, library, or office.

I hope this book will serve as a source of inspiration and a tool for looking at color with a new eye. If there is one thing we've learned at *Southern Accents,* it's that photography alters colors and so does light. A room that looks soft green in the morning may look almost chartreuse at night under artificial light. A room with white walls may turn slightly yellow depending on the position of the sun and, in the pages of the magazine, because of the color shifts at our printer. You will find many tidbits of information in this book, but one to take with you is this: if you respond to a color in a book or magazine, take the image with you to the paint store or your paint consultant or your designer. It's the best way to get a match. The back of the book includes information about designers, as well as a list of paint manufacturers to get you started.

When we survey our readers, they regularly rate those homes that meld color and tradition and comfort over those that seem more monochromatic or modern. I think we all take comfort in color and tradition. And since homes are as much havens as habitats these days, coloring them takes on an importance that transcends trends.

chapter 1

Blues

The color blue has been associated with just about every fashion trend in history. There was the European craze for Chinese blue-and-white export porcelain, Delft, and Staffordshire pottery; the icy blue of Art Deco; the indigo blue that made Levi jeans an icon and a statement in one. At the beginning of this century, robin's-egg-blue upholstery, with its soft tones, got a lot of ink in the design press. In its infinite variations, blue always creates a buzz. Symbolically, it signifies constancy. Think of the phrase "true blue friend." In its translucent form, it conveys an openness and clarity that let interior spaces breathe.

Blue's versatility and changeability make it perennially popular. It can be bright or sedate, traditional or ultramodern, classic or totally trendy. It is the nuance of this (and every) color that makes it a success, but the richness of blue almost guarantees a compelling interior, whether on a small or large scale.

Throughout history, shades of blue have appeared in rich ceramic tiles in Italy, Morocco, England, and America as well as in Matisse's cutouts and Picasso's blue period, the abstract expressionist paintings of Wassily Kandinsky, and the sensual sculptures of Yves Klein. All of those works and so many more set a standard for the reproduction of blue. Used in concert with other colors, blue invokes more than just admiration; it also evokes a sense of place. Light blue and white make us think of Swedish Neoclassicism. Grouped with strong pinks and greens, blue elicits Indian or Moroccan styles. Blue and brown bring to mind Indonesian batiks, while red, white, and blue make us feel patriotic. And, of course, baby blue seems utterly appropriate in a newborn boy's nursery.

Despite its beauty, blue is also associated with a rich American musical tradition that finds its inspiration in despair. American writer Washington Irving is credited with having coined the term *the blues,* but its melancholy connotations date back to the Elizabethan era. While it's difficult to comprehend how a clear blue sky might inspire misery, with more opaque shades — royal, navy — which seem close cousins to black, this idea makes more sense. Either way, blue, like any color, is not for everybody all the

PAGE XIV: In an Atlanta bedroom, a softened blue-and-white toile de Jouy covers the bed, the bench, and the club chair. Designer Jackye Lanham trimmed the corners in fringe that picks up the color scheme but keeps it understated.

PAGE 1 AND BELOW: A Venetian mirror hanging over an antique French chest of drawers conveys a sense of cool elegance. The floral painting and rococo curves on the mirror and commode reflect the lush environment reflected in the mirror.

BELOW: The absence of a rug and the cool blue walls make this Dallas space look fairly modern in spirit. But it is actually historically, colorfully correct and full of antiques — notice the French bergères, the petit gueridon table before the fireplace, the gilt mirror and mantel garniture, and the elegant fabrics.

OPPOSITE: Cool and warm elements combine in the living room. The blue walls give life to the collection of drawings hung from silver hardware, while the honey-toned wood and yellow and violet print on the sofa warm up the composition and keep the room inviting as well as beautiful.

OPPOSITE: Blue makes it into the bedroom, where order and antiques promise a restful night's sleep. The cool color almost becomes a neutral that lets the patina of paint on the headboard and wood in the Empire nightstand, roll-top secretary, and Directoire fauteuil stand out. The white bedcover lends a crisp contrast.

RIGHT: A soft blue that almost appears gray provides the backdrop to a pair of antique creamware cups and saucers. The contrast between the white tablecloth, the cream-colored ceramics, and the painted blue wood behind keep the presentation as subtle as it is sophisticated.

time. Virginia designer Barry Dixon uses blues sparingly in his projects: "The temperature goes down five degrees in a blue room," he says, "and it can be unflattering to skin."

In the Deep South, a cool color is often welcome. "I love blue: it cools things off," says Atlanta designer Jackye Lanham. "Think about where we are. It's the South. It's hot. A little fresh color goes a long way down here." Blue is particularly prevalent in coastal locations. Whether in Palm Beach or on the coast of the Carolinas, soft blues seem to cool a hot August afternoon. Of course, it's all about perspective. In cooler climates, such as Virginia, where winter takes temperatures below freezing for at least two months, there is more reluctance to use blues. Therefore, Dixon works with warmer shades — "robin's-egg blue, celadon blue/green, and that great color you get when you fill a bathtub with water."

Blue seems a simplistic term to contain all the many variations of the shade. From icy blue to aqua, teal to periwinkle, blue's many identities can go on ad infinitum. Designers William Diamond and Anthony Barrata decorated an entire house in tints of blue, where the contrasts were clear and crisp. The clever marketing departments at Crayola Crayons, J. Crew clothing, even paint manufacturers have made the distinctions more challenging. One person's seafoam is another person's teal, and so on.

Adam Blue and Periwinkle

Robin's-egg blue may be the color of the moment, but the most classic hue is Adam blue, inspired by the eighteenth-century interiors of Scottish architect Robert Adam. He designed spaces that were grand, elegant, and a little imposing. The popularity of the color may have something to do with the timelessness of his designs. Neoclassical in style, Adam's designs in architecture and furniture are imitated to this day. An Atlanta house designed by Jackye Lanham makes a thoughtful nod to Adam with softly tinted blue walls, accented by Regency furniture. Natural light warms any hint of an icy feeling.

Wedgwood blue is a close cousin to the shade used often by Robert Adam. It describes the color of ceramics, called jasperware, designed by Josiah Wedgwood in the eighteenth century. The textured surface proved ideal for white relief decorations that mimicked plaster architectural reliefs Adam installed in his houses. In plates, platters, vases, and medallions, blue jasperware responded to the desires of a new elite middle class. Jasperware's blue color is reproduced today, and collectors still seek out original eighteenth-century examples. The reproductions are so plentiful that we almost take for granted the remarkable beauty of Wedgwood blue.

The blue that has almost become the navy blue of the twenty-first century seems to be periwinkle. It is easy on the eyes and coordinates with crisp whites and khaki browns. It suggests a casual spirit that can be subtly formalized on silk. It has warmth, colored

OPPOSITE: The contrast of black and gold — in the Regency chairs, the sconces, the frames — enhances the cool tones in the soft blue walls.

OPPOSITE: On Sea Island in Georgia, designer John Oetgen has created a fresh escape with the combination of blue-and-white-stripe and periwinkle chair upholstery set off by white walls and brown wood on the furniture and the ceiling beams. The furniture arrangement is intimate, but the architecture of the room keeps the space feeling airy and cool.

RIGHT: A contemporary Tibetan carpet warms an intimate spot in Sea Island, and the blue upholstery gives the space a strong accent of color. The botanical watercolors on the wall evoke the tropical landscape outside without the tangle of overgrowth.

as it is by the addition of a little red to bring it closer to lavender, and it conveys depth.

On the coast in Georgia, Atlanta designer John Oetgen chose a light, simple palette accented by periwinkle to amplify the spaces in a Mediterranean-style villa. In the central living area, he upholstered antique English wing chairs in that color. The matching sofas are covered with a periwinkle-and-white stripe. The only other strong colors are shades of brown — in the ceiling beams and fans, the furniture, the frames around the art. The deep brown brings the blue down to earth a bit, making the whole arrangement seem less ethereal.

Oetgen played with blue again in a sitting area off the entry hall, this time incorporating a deeper, brighter blue. In both areas, accents of green — the dining chairs next to the living area and the botanical watercolors in the sitting area — are reminders that the house is at the beach and surrounded by a verdant landscape.

BELOW: Variations on blue — from periwinkle to cobalt to aqua — fill this grand Palm Beach living room designed by New York designers William Diamond and Anthony Baratta. The custom woven rug integrates all of the shades.

OPPOSITE: The dining room chairs, covered in a custom check, are five feet tall. The walls are covered in aqua linen. "We like to have fabrics custom-dyed so that we can control the color," explains William Diamond.

Aqua

A house in Palm Beach, outfitted in a range of blues in preppy plaids and stylish geo-metrics on everything from rugs to upholstery to light fixtures, provides a cool visual respite when the heat of the coast overpowers. The shades of blue and light green seem harvested from the waters beyond. Brown wood and white walls are the accents, but blue dominates. In the great room, a robin's-egg blue sofa is flanked by a club chair and camelback sofa upholstered in a soft aquatic blue-green. The two colors are brought together by the area rug, which has geometric shapes that include both tones as well as white. The vastness of the space evokes the endless sky and ocean, frequent sights at coastal locations. The same palette recurs in the dining room, the bedrooms, and the entry, all with different decorative approaches that still embrace the same atti-tude — elegance that reflects the casual spirit of the coast. "The house may look mon-otone," says William Diamond of the design team Diamond Baratta, "but it's actually the highest contrast within one hue, from the reddest blue — periwinkle — to the yellowest blue — aqua."

Another house in Palm Beach, a pool house by Swedish Palm Beach designer Lars Bolander, looks out open doorways to a landscape of green foliage and an aqua pool. In the living area, he used white cotton canvas and a woven water hyacinth sofa and chairs as a neutral counterpoint to the views through the walls. Cobalt towels draped across a chair connect the interior rooms to the blue water beyond. Bolander's facility with blue is probably as much a part of his heritage as his design talent. The palette of his native Sweden makes one immediately think of luminescent blues and grays. The same aesthetic works well in Florida. "I love gray blues, soft colors, really," says Bolander. "But it all really depends on the project. You may work with the landscape. You may transcend it. It's up to the client." Bolander could have incorporated the palette of the outdoors in the pool house. Even with open walls that look out to the surrounding landscape, this pool house provides a cool retreat from its tropical set-ting, a clear division, within easy access.

OPPOSITE: A pressed-tin ceiling and subway tile lend restaurant polish to the well-equipped kitchen. The insides of the lighting fixtures are painted aqua to give interest and color to an area often overlooked.

Cobalt towels draped across white canvas cushions
make a connection to the saturated green of the Palm
Beach landscape and the pool's aqua-colored water.

Turquoise

Charleston designer Amelia Handegan often uses a palette that's as sedate as it is rich. She enlivens the arrangement with shots of strong color — blues, pinks, greens. In one bedroom she designed, she draped a turquoise-colored Indian silk sari with woven silver motifs across the end of a bed. Other more muted shades of blue show up in a throw pillow on the bed and as upholstery on a side chair. But the room does not feel "blue"; Handegan has imposed balance between a strong shade and muted neutrals where neither overtakes. Handegan says, "Never think 'match'; think relationship, intensity, value." The more muted blues tone down the brighter shades, and they are all warmed up a bit by the use of brown — on tailored window treatments, a mahogany bed frame, old plank flooring. "The different intense blues used in the bedroom are close to each other. The textures — silk, glass, painting — allow the shades to molt together," she says. Each item is a bit of punctuation in an otherwise green room. "Take away the blues, and the room would be almost monochromatic." Handegan attributes the room's success to the tension the colors inspire. "They create energy," she says.

The house's entry hall received the same shot of energy when Handegan created colorful cushions for a pair of Regency chairs. As we all know, the entry should be inviting, an indicator of tastes and personality, so a neutral space might suggest that you desire serenity, while a room with color implies that you are open to excitement as well. In the entry hall on page xi the abstract painting reveals the owner's taste in art, the delicate chairs reflect an appreciation for classic lines and refinement, and the turquoise cushions help bring the little space to life.

OPPOSITE: A neutral bedroom gets a hint of drama from the Indian silk sari at the end of the bed. Blue accents help direct the eye around the room, from the sari and chair covers to the accent pillow to the light blue painted nightstands and painting.

Cerulean

The most ever-present color in the South — aside from the green landscape that surrounds us — is the clear blue of the sky overhead. In the heat of August or the cool of January, the sky provides unceasing inspiration. It's a hopeful color but rather strong in its purest form. Toned down a bit, it makes a wonderful reference to the environment. Variations evoke the sky, and placement reinforces the reference — on ceilings, canopies, trim, and moldings. Because it's such an easy shade to live with, it works as a complement to other blues throughout the room. Chicago designer Alessandra Branca calls cerulean blue one of her favorite colors. "It's just beautiful," she says. "It reverberates. It intensifies depending on the setting."

What attracts Birmingham designer Phillip Sides to cerulean is that "sky blue is not blue blue," he says. "It's actually more lavender. It's got some red in it, so it's not cold." Sides used cerulean on the ceiling in a house he designed at Rosemary Beach, Florida. The color on the ceiling also relates to a blue sectional in the neighboring living area and periwinkle accents in the study across the hall. Even though the blues do not match, the ceiling color connects the rooms without making the design scheme seem contrived. The soaring vaulted ceiling refers to the sky outside in the same way the decor of the entire house reflects the environment at Rosemary Beach.

OPPOSITE: The canopy's lining suggests the sky. Throughout the room, touches of soft blue — in the bedside tables, the chair covers, the art — extend the shade beyond the canopy.

In a Rosemary Beach house by Phillip Sides, a not-so-subtle reference to the coastal Florida landscape. A sunny yellow checked fabric diffuses light that bathes the aqua sectional in warmth. Across the hall in the study, saturated blues and browns in the curtains can block out coastal light. The hall ceiling ties all the blues together.

Cobalt

Away from the coast it is fairly rare to see blue as a dominant color. As an accent, however, colors like cobalt, royal, or navy blue provide a striking visual contrast. In Rome, Jo Bettoja, a Georgia-born former model and now a cookbook author, sets a stylish table with cobalt glasses. In a room full of color and light, the cobalt stands out and provides a counterpoint to everything else. The plates look whiter, the silver more brilliant, the linens fresher. The cobalt glasses also bring the many colors of the room together — the paintings, upholstery, accessories.

In a Dallas bedroom, white stripes lighten a strong marine blue and a more exotic pattern draped from the corona and lying across the bed, as well as the scalloped borders around the pillows. The patterns also keep the room from feeling static. The colors and the combinations are so strong that throwing another shade into the mix would throw off the elegant balance.

OPPOSITE: Red reappears in the chair upholstery, the clothing in the paintings, even the hue of the antique wood furniture, but it is the color in the cobalt glasses that helps to animate the room.

LEFT: Were this bedroom just about blue-and-white stripes, it might seem tailor-made for a man, but with the addition of scalloped trim on the pillows and the dramatic silk and silver fabric draped from the corona, the bedroom seems suited for a woman too.

Blue and White

It may seem strange to label a color combination as a color, but the two are ubiquitous as paired tones — and they make a strong enough showing in *Southern Accents* to merit sizable mention in this book. On ceramics the colors can be precious, as in the Chinese export porcelain that made its way to Europe in the fourteenth century. Or they may be as unpretentious as the simply thrown pieces that fill the shelves of your neighborhood Pier 1. From $3 to $300,000, blue-and-white porcelain and pottery have enchanted for centuries. The blue in the porcelain came from cobalt, which has a long and distinguished history. Traced to ancient Egypt and Persia, it came into its own in thirteenth century China.

Blue-and-white porcelain wares launched an aesthetic that endures to this day. Full of treachery and triumph, the history of the production, export, and imitation of blue-and-white porcelain and pottery goes deep.

Blue and white's decorative role doesn't end with pretty pottery. There is blue-and-white toile de Jouy, the patterned fabric that became almost de rigueur in fine Southern interiors in the 1990s, as well as many other print and stripe incarnations. As accents in a room, blue and white will dominate. The pairing softens the combination of two rather harsh colors — it almost reads as a more interesting light blue. There is something utterly dynamic about the combination of the two colors, of the play between the clarity of one and the richness of the other.

OPPOSITE: Delft tiles inspired the design of the carpet in the master bedroom, where patterns, stripes, florals, and solids all reflect a profound love of color.

BELOW: Walnut wood reflects the patina of blue-and-white Chinese export porcelain. The neutral space remains understated even though the porcelain urns are boldly colored.

OPPOSITE: The combination of blue and white on pottery and porcelain has captivated for centuries. A collection of fine and not-so-fine plates can fill a whole wall with strong color without overwhelming the space.

Bedrooms, powder rooms, children's rooms — essentially intimate spaces — are frequently the setting for blue-and-white toile de Jouy. Most toile de Jouy is not fine silk but rather cotton or linen, not always the material selected for public spaces. Also, the scenes depicted on toile de Jouy are petite and personal — a farm, garden, or even tropical scene with children or animals playing together. For many of us, toile de Jouy is one of those fabrics that inspire true love. The more of it the better. It might be a little overwhelming in a large space that is visited often. But in a bedroom on walls, ceilings, bedcovers, or headboards, it's a comforting presence — hearkening back to the eighteenth-century when fabric manufacturers first started producing it — and enduringly stylish.

With ceramics as well, an attraction to more over less prevails. Collections of plates and platters and tiles that cover backsplashes and surround fireplaces fill homes from western Europe to south Texas. A collection is easy to acquire, particularly if you don't mind that the plates or tiles don't match. Countries like Greece, Portugal, Holland, France, England, Germany, and Spain, as well as China and Japan, have all produced blue-and-white wares at one time or another. While entire sets of plates may be difficult and expensive to get your hands on, the odd antique plate found here or there can become a rewarding, easily portable souvenir. In addition, there are numerous inexpensive reproductions available in home design shops. Covering walls, filling breakfronts, or even sitting on a tabletop, a vast collection of blue-and-white ceramics coordinates with almost every color — taupe, more white, purple, yellow, green, more blue, orange. It is, essentially, the "no-brainer" color combination — working in whatever form it takes.

The collection of blue-and-white Chinese export porcelain is so exquisite on its own that an overly wrought floral arrangement would have taken away from the table setting. These pieces are part of the well-known Hatcher collection. On this table, Chinese silver-and-blue tea paper on the walls picks up the blue, and the lavender flowers give a sense of freshness to the four-hundred-year-old porcelain.

Purple

One of our most popular magazine covers of late featured a bedroom in Charleston, South Carolina, designed by Amelia Handegan. A source of extensive debate among the staff because purple seemed a risk as a cover choice, the image garnered positive responses and the risk paid off. The purple spoke to readers, as did the elements of the carefully constructed room. "Lavender is not as definite a color as purple," says Handegan. "Its paleness is probably what appeals to people."

Violet and lavender: the histories of the colors are as long as those of the plants of the same names. Their associations are numerous. Purple is the color of royalty; violet symbolized delicacy. And of course there is the more recent incarnation of purple in the psychedelic '60s and '70s. In the Charleston bedroom, Handegan took traditional patterns — plaids, toiles, and prints — and put them together within this seemingly singular color palette. The palette ended up looking neither magisterial nor off-putting, nor did it get its inspiration from the "purple haze" of decades past. It was fresh, inspired by nature, but clearly mastered by a hand adept at balancing color, form, and pattern.

Handegan decided on lavender for the bedroom "after finding an antique fragment of toile de Jouy in deep purple that depicted Diana the Huntress," she says. "The pale lavender actually works as a counterpoint to the deep purple hues" in the archival fabric. She covered a pair of stools in lavender toile de Jouy. The large-checked fabric provided the ideal contrast — a bold pattern in a soft hue. The purples and the colors of the painted surfaces are pulled together in the print fabric on the side chair, which has touches of a mint green that share the same intensity as the purple but introduce another complementary color. "Many colors could be used with lavender," she says. "I prefer cocoa or neutral colors. I just think it's more sophisticated than pastels."

Of course, flowers are what most often come to mind when thinking about purple. There are so many varieties — muscari, hyacinth, anemone, lavender, lilac, hydrangea,

tulip, violet, pansy, iris — the list seems limitless. Each flower has its attraction, but the reason that these blossoms are so universally popular has to do with their season of bloom: spring. Even on fabrics, purple is most often grouped with the colors of spring — green, white, yellow, pink, blue. It's hard to imagine such a pale palette in a wintry wood-paneled library with a fire roaring below the mantel.

However, purple metamorphoses when you group it to bring out its more baroque personality. Arranged with red or raspberry — deep colors, without an easygoing pastel in sight — purple takes on a much more serious tone, becoming downright somber if used in large quantities. Royal purple seems as full of drama as the monarchies of centuries past. In its freshest incarnation, purple seems most akin to blue — clear and yet somehow warm. In its deepest coloration — it is a close cousin to black — serious, quiet, perhaps menacing. "I hate dark purple," says designer Alessandra Branca. "But lavender, like a lavender-and-yellow toile, is another thing altogether."

A renewed national appreciation for the pale version of purple has made it one of the "hot" new colors on the market today. "I love lavender," says Atlanta designer Jackye Lanham. "And I also like the purpley color you see on Famille Rose porcelain — it's mauve, in a good way," she says, referring to the dusty purple/pink that became the shade of choice in chain hotel rooms across the country in the 1980s. Lanham anticipates coordinating lavender with a slightly toned-down apple green to create a new classic pairing.

At the dawn of the twenty-first century, it seems as though we've all arrived at the realization that pale does not imply puny. "Loud, strong color wears on the psyche," says Phillip Sides. With so much external stimulation and a renewed emphasis on taking care of the home, it seems likely that the new colors will be much like the old ones — variations on Robert Adam's and Josiah Wedgwood's soft shades, pretty purples, and the occasional shot of cobalt.

PAGE 33: A fragment of a dark purple toile de Jouy inspired Amelia Handegan's design for this bedroom. She lightened the palette and introduced the bold check and a multicolored print on the chair to tie the colors together.

RIGHT: The deep purple brings out the subtle red hues in the wood. Because the room is small, the crown moldings are painted purple as well, presumably to make it feel larger. The ceiling is terra-cotta color and casts a warming glow about the room.

On the Color Wheel

It's impossible to discuss color without mentioning the "color wheel." A circle of colors that is as much instinctive as learned, it shows, in its coloration, the relationship between shades. Organized so that two primary colors (yellow, red, blue) are separated by secondary colors (orange, violet, green), the wheel serves as a tool in color planning.

Complementary colors are those that are opposite each other on the wheel — green and red, yellow and lavender, blue and orange — and they will always work well together. Think of your garden and what flowers you group in your seasonal planting. Also, neighboring colors work well together. Blue and lavender are next to each other on the

wheel, and they often show up together in floral and garden arrangements and in interiors.

Experienced interior designers rarely consult a color wheel. Their knowledge of the variations in color and shade are so ingrained, they're instinctive. And designers do not follow the rules of the color wheel either. "I try to consciously clash color," says Birmingham designer Phillip Sides. "Look out the window. There are more greens out there and other colors that don't match one another, that shouldn't be together. But they are, and that's what happens in nature. A medley of complementary and clashing colors is what makes a house real. It takes the stiffness out of an arrangement. It's just not so matchy matchy."

sample swatches:

"I've always believed that people gravitate toward colors that appear in the pigment of the eyes. Blue is a very cool color, but when it's offset with a warm brown and straw it is very flattering and comfortable." – JACQUELYNNE P. LANHAM

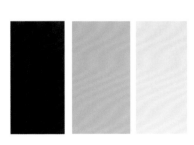

sample swatches:

" I love a calm and serene color palette in beautiful shades of blue, blue-green – mixed with luscious shades of cream and beige, in various and different fabrics and textures. The result is soothing and elegant." — GERRIE BREMERMANN

chapter 2

Greens

In the South, green has a long history in our interiors. Our agrarian past connects us to the landscape, almost inextricably. Generations ago, houses had no central air, so large open windows facilitated enough breeze to keep the air moving. Those windows looked out to a tableau of green trees and cut flower, vegetable, and herb gardens, providing a landscape few paintings could match. In fact, when interior designs are conceived, many factors influence color choices — light, shadow, mood, and the view through the window — which may explain why there is such diversity in the interior greens that you see in *Southern Accents*. Sage, celadon, moss, and chartreuse are just a few of the colors that have made their way into our interiors. Nature is so integral to coloring a space, designers are always on the lookout for inspiration. Barry Dixon lets a client's relationship with nature influence the greens he'll use in an interior. "If a client loves summer, then I'll use summer greens and the colors of different flowers that grow during summer. Spring is more pastel — lighter greens and pinks. And of course fall has the warmer, earthier colors."

Designers are attuned to color in ways that the average person is not. We can go outside and recognize a beautiful day, but it is only the truly observant who will recognize the components of the day that make it so compelling. Jennifer Garrigues says, "Outside there are so many wonderful landscapes, and green is the backdrop for most of them. Green is calming and has a feeling of nature. People don't often see green outside, so I bring it in." They take it for granted. But pulled inside, away from its natural environment, green has a personality all its own.

From the bold kelly greens that appear on floral-printed chintzes to subtle limestone and mint and vibrant chartreuse, green is chameleonlike in its ability to take on alternate identities. Wassily Kandinsky called green the "bourgeoisie." Considered restful, passive, even wearisome, green absorbs the coolness of blue and the warmth of yellow that combine to form it. At the same time it is the color associated with the fiery Irish and a holy color among the Islamic. It is also considered the color of jealousy, a sentiment that stirs passions and incites betrayal. It transcends trends, and yet when we talk about what's in or out in relation to color, green does have a few shades in the "out" category: hunter and teal, to name two. Overused in the 1980s, they make most of us avert our eyes today. But it's the concept more than the color that is most objectionable — those heavy plaids and prints that made no room for light and warmth. Seen in the context of contemporary designs, each of those colors can be rich and stylish. At its most fundamental, green can be a color of controversy, but it conveys a stillness and calm that seem at home in the interiors that have appeared in the pages of *Southern Accents.*

PAGE 38: The wall acts as a large mat, pulling in the fifteen prints of historic interiors so that the arrangement can be read as a single, grand work of art. Green leather with gilt details reiterates the color in the walls.

BELOW: Dreaded by some because of its dated associations, teal is still a classic color, particularly when used with something historical. The seventeenth-century French tapestry inspired the choice of teal fabric under the canopy.

OPPOSITE: Birmingham architect Bill Ingram relaxed a deep gray green in the kitchen with the addition of the green plaid upholstery on the antique stools. Steel appliances bring out the gray.

LEFT: A mint green bedroom in Palm Beach designed by Kemble Interiors catches the afternoon breezes. The choice of a single color — even though it appears on the floor in checks, in stripes on the wall, and in a pattern on the linens — gives the room a sense of peace and coherence.

BELOW: In the whimsical Palm Beach living room, French doors provide the transition between walls covered in a pomegranate print and the exterior garden with its lush tropical foliage.

Sage Green

Easy on the eyes, almost textural in its softness, sage and celadon bring to mind compatible images. On walls, dressing windows, atop furnishings or tables, these greens evoke the earth without getting dingy. As at home with crisp white linen or rich chocolate, celadon is versatile and subtle, and it often evolves with the light — becoming beige in the morning light and even greener lit by yellow cast lamplight. What makes the colors so easy to live with are the gray tones that soften sage, the subtle browns that make celadon rich. Both appeal to those of us who love color but resist bright shades. "It's really a gray-green," says Phillip Sides. "And it can easily become a neutral."

Atlanta designer Jackye Lanham finds inspiration for the sage, celadon palette she lives with in her husband's collection of globes. "There's a parchment color I love, the blue-green of the waters, the soft green of the land. They're all so inspirational," she says. A striking backdrop to creamware, antique portraits, shagreen boxes, magnifying glasses, and the like, green speaks personally to Lanham. And she maintains variations on the palette throughout her house, intensifying or softening it depending on the light or function of a room.

Her dining room is enveloped in a sage linen velvet that becomes almost taupe in contrast to the vibrant greens outside her windows. The deeper green velvet covering the dining table pulls the green in from the outside and refers back to the walls. A floral arrangement with greenery cut from the garden underscores the color scheme in the room.

A recent addition to Lanham's house, what she calls the "stone room," connects the kitchen and dining room. It reflects a masterful integration of materials and environment — indoors and out. Oak beams, Georgia granite, French limestone on the floor are all drawn directly from nature. Abundant windows in the room let light in to warm the space and eliminate the need for any art. Turned oak, walnut, and mahogany wood furniture provide a contrast with the rustic materials. But it's the sage velvet on the sofa and ottoman that mediate the tension between the gray of the walls and flooring and the lush green trees and lawns.

PAGE 44: In Jackye Lanham's Atlanta garden room, sage upholstery reflects the green of the outdoors and the gray in the stone floors and walls. The dark wood furniture and rough-hewn beams pull the arrangement together.

BELOW: A toned-down celadon serves as a neutral backdrop to a pale yellow sofa from the 1940s, and keeps the mood of this Dallas living room light.

OPPOSITE: Linen velvet walls surround Lanham's dining room, where a mahogany and burled elm sideboard and ebony Regency chairs provide a natural contrast. A collection of crystal adds translucent elegance.

BELOW: Jackye Lanham finds inspiration for her old-world color schemes in the collections she shares with her husband: antique magnifying glasses, globes, tortoiseshell, and books.

OPPOSITE: The antique Oriental carpet provided the inspiration for the earth tones in this New Orleans library. Green in the silk window treatments and the velvet upholstery on the canapé and on the fauteuils complements the rich brown of the walnut wood.

Birmingham architect Bill Ingram is known for his balancing of furniture and art, interior design and architecture in homes that are best described as "classic modern." He respects the lessons of the past, particularly those of the Georgian era, but his interest in clean lines, spare settings, and subtle colors makes his projects feel modern.

The palette Ingram works with often is a soft gray green. It appears throughout all the living areas in his house. His reason? "Greens are calming," he says. "Even apple green." In Ingram's house, the gray-green works as a neutral accent. It's a foil in his interiors, as cypress doors, mahogany and walnut antique furniture, and soft pastel silks and linens vie for attention and always come out even.

OPPOSITE: Peach tones in the upholstery and even in the book spines complement the rich celadon Chinese urns. The green color stands out against the neutral walls and console.

ABOVE: In Jackye Lanham's master bedroom, calming sage green glows under the light cast by luminescent linen window treatments.

Moss

While we like to think that we're immune to trends, there has been a definite awakening to the versatility and livability of sage in the last few years. It seems like one of those colors immune to overuse. And that may just be the nature of green and its varying shades. It is so easygoing that by adding or subtracting gray, yellow, or brown, it takes on new identities. One color that has been around for centuries and through cultures is a mossy shade of green. A true green that can rarely if ever be mistaken for another color, no matter the light, moss is more akin to the original colors that covered walls in colonial America.

While style evolves over time and most interior designs adapt as tastes change, there are those elements that are timeless, and moss green, like yellow or red, is one color that stands the test of time. In a period interior or one completed yesterday, moss can look equally correct and chic. The accents are what make the difference. Memphis designer William Eubanks upholstered the furniture in his morning room a green velvet. The color stands out in the oak-paneled room, making a reference to the outdoors. "Because of their rainy days, the English painted their public rooms vibrant reds, blues, yellows, and greens," says Eubanks, "to juxtapose with the gray weather outdoors." Throughout the room, spots of green reiterate the color on the sofa.

In Dallas, Paul Garzotto painted a library an unexpected moss color. The vast room showcases a collection of art, globes, books, ceramics, and furniture. Light streams in through curtained windows. Green leather and velvet seating offer comfortable, stylish spots for reading. The green color is dark enough to be serious but not so somber that the pleasures of a well-lit, airy library get lost in the design.

OPPOSITE: In a large living area, a composition of antique drawings framed in gold surround a moss velvet-covered antique French fauteuil. The tones of the art, the frames, the wood, and the upholstery all suggest a mellow patina of age and character.

BELOW: A centuries-old technique of painting gold onto porcelain, encrustation often pairs the most regal colors. In this instance, gold and green seem destined to decorate an elegant tabletop.

OPPOSITE: The moss green on the sofa and the tapestry upholstery on the wing chairs serve as a serene counterpoint to the rich reds and golds in William Eubanks's morning room.

RIGHT: A painted Louis XVI side chair is upholstered in a moss green antique velvet. Once probably more opaque, the faded velvet seems appropriate to an antique fabric that has endured the New Orleans sun.

BELOW: While the only color in libraries usually comes from book spines, this room is full of color, pattern, and light and is still conducive to reading. Painted in fifteen coats of color and glaze, the moss tone on the walls reappears in the curtains, the upholstery, even the porcelain collection.

OPPOSITE: A famille vert vase on a gueridon table in the library provides a reference point for the green on the walls in the rest of the room.

Foliage

While it's virtually impossible to replicate the green of the outdoors — the waxy surface that makes leaves glow, the rich texture that gives depth — there is no end to papers and fabrics and paints that approximate the color with remarkable accuracy. From Palm Beach to Dallas, floral chintzes sport colors of the outdoors that capture the intensity of flowers and greenery. Prints of ferns and other leaves seem to be particularly popular. Years ago, one fabric manufacturer produced an ivy print that still shows up in everything from bedrooms to hotel powder rooms.

It is rare to find kelly green as an overall shade because it is so vibrant. When it's softened with a bit of yellow and creamy white, it often becomes more chartreuse. Chinese artisans who created pure red, blue, yellow, and green porcelains, among others, got the true color and incorporated it in wares of such simple beauty that they capture astonishing prices on the antiques market today. Later, European porcelain factories incorporated rich colors in their creations but never with the same intensity as the Chinese. However, these pieces are accessories, and it is rare to see pure green in its entirety on anything grander than a pillow. The color is just too strong. Think of the outdoors and all the variations of green. Were foliage all the same color, it would be not only boring but utterly overwhelming.

As a print, however, foliage-themed fabrics and papers cover walls and furniture with equal aplomb. Palm Beach designers like Brooke Huttig and Mimi McMakin pull out the subtlest touches from the print, reds and browns and variations on the green, to make lively living spaces that are as vibrant as the exterior gardens in the tony community.

Swedish designer Lars Bolander, whose signature palette runs more along Gustavian lines, created a terrace setting in Palm Beach that looks inspired more by Bali

PAGE 58: At the Palm Beach home of Lars Bolander, the terrace is awash with bold, tropical colors. Because Bolander is Swedish and his work is most often associated with a Gustavian palette, his choice of bold color here is a surprise. "You can work with your surroundings or transcend them. In my house, I chose to work with them," he says.

LEFT: The Chinese porcelain bowl reflects the early artisan's ability to work with pure color. French gilders would have added the gilt or ormolu mounts after the bowl arrived in France.

RIGHT: Nineteenth-century Vieux Paris gumbo bowls bordered in a bright green lend a fresh take on green to a holiday tabletop, proving that red and green — traditional Christmas colors — need not be dowdy.

OPPOSITE: Inspired by the Arts and Crafts movement, the wallpaper in the dining room of this Virginia house serves as a patterned foil to designer J. R. Miller's collection of maritime paintings. The gilt frames and the blue skies bring out those shades in the paper.

than by Northern Europe. A print featuring great elephant ear leaves covers green painted wicker furniture. Palm plants, pink bougainvillea, and hibiscus take the palette up a notch, and a sun umbrella fringed in yellow suggests the hottest tropics. In this case, Lars is living among his south Florida surroundings, embracing the tropical climate rather than defying it.

Lighter prints that take the intensity of green foliage down a bit appear in toile de Jouy and fern prints, which seem to be attracting a lot of attention right now. The fern-printed paper and fabrics resemble pressed ferns or the illustrated prints that came out of antique horticultural volumes. They bear the softness of age and fading and are easier on the eye. Toile de Jouy, with its pastoral scenes, shows up often in green variations, where the green is softened by its companion ecru, making it ideal for a bedroom or garden room. It is not a color you want to see everywhere, so a single room or corner is an ideal spot for a bit of this kind of outdoor color.

OPPOSITE: This Dallas pool house has all the elegance of a grand estate, but moss-green-stained concrete floors and vinylized fern-patterned linen on the chairs make the space grandchildren-friendly. The doors to the house open to the pool and the garden not far beyond.

ABOVE, LEFT: In the South, the relationship between the inside and out is inextricable. To underscore it, designers often select fabrics with natural motifs. Here an arrangement that looks as if it were cut from flowers beyond the door sits atop an antique bamboo coffee table. The green floral motif on the fabric echoes the greenery beyond.

ABOVE, RIGHT: A pretty green-and-white toile contrasts with a Victorian mahogany headboard and gives the feeling of a very sophisticated tree house. A trumeau peers through the open headboard and reflects the window in front of the bed.

Chartreuse

A few years ago, the magazine received a letter complaining that that there were too many green apples in our photographs. While it may have been true to some extent, our defense was that they provide a fresh shot of color that contrasts particularly well with saturated shades like blue and white, yellow, even pink. And the color injects some much-needed energy into otherwise neutral rooms.

Since then, fabric, tableware, and paint manufacturers have embraced apple green with a vengeance. A close cousin to yellow, chartreuse mimics those shades that fill our springtime and summer gardens. The longevity of this trend is assured. Chartreuse works as a counterpoint to fall colors and enlivens the dreariest winter rooms. It can even take the traditional red and green of the holidays and give it a lively twist. Bill Ingram says, "You wouldn't think a gray green and yellow green can look great together, but it works." He used an apple green in the light-filled second-floor bedroom of a Birmingham house, and the room functioned as a beacon from almost all the other subtly colored spaces. A color once thought garish is turning out to be a very versatile shade.

At Rosemary Beach, Birmingham designer Phillip Sides incorporated chartreuse throughout a guesthouse. The inspiration started with contemporary vases and ran through upholstery and even bold horizontal stripes on the wall. Sides allowed the chartreuse to be the dominant, rather than the accent, color. He used a soft white as a contrast and then toned down the chartreuse so it was less Day-Glo than stem fresh. No matter the weather outside, a bright beachy day or a stormy afternoon, the chartreuse will stay warm and inviting, happy and evocative of its coastal setting. "It's actually one of my favorite spaces in that house," says Sides. "It's a fun room but it's also calm. I creamed the chartreuse a bit and it's actually really soft." Because we are surrounded by so much greenery, particularly in the South, it is refreshing to bring in one shade or a few variations, to pull them out of their environment and give them new life and a new look in an interior. Green may be a calm, restful color, but it will also always suggest vitality because its inspiration is all about life and growth.

PAGE 65: At the home of designer Herbert Wells, soft green-apple on the walls of the Houston, Texas, dining room evolves with the light of the day. The walnut wood of the two French cabinets, with their honey color, brings out the yellow in the walls.

BELOW: The guest cottage at Rosemary Beach is actually an efficiency, where the living room sofa pulls out and transforms the room into a bedroom. Phillip Sides found inspiration for the chartreuse color in the natural environment, and he ran it through the space. Horizontal stripes make the room look broader. The artwork on the walls is reflected in the fabric on the pillows.

The chartreuse color that Sides used might have been as intense as the vases on the demilune table, but he "creamed it up a bit" so that the intensity would be easier on the eye. Yellow, cream, and black accents soften the ensemble.

LEFT: Green that goes from pale to chartreuse with the advancing hours of the day envelops a Birmingham master bedroom in color. The bed linens are the most neutral yellow. Designer Phillip Sides chose a floral print to line the inside of the canopy, to give the room pattern without overwhelming it. The accent of black in the bedstead gives definition to the canopy, which functions as a sort of room within a room.

BELOW: The bathroom in the Birmingham house is actually painted the same color as the bedroom, but the light makes it look chartreuse.

A toned-down chartreuse gets its inspiration from the multicolored toile de Jouy on the pillows and windows. The playfully shaped headboard seems in keeping with the wall color and fabric.

OPPOSITE: In a Dallas dining room, apple green on the walls contrasts with window treatments that let in light. Cream-colored architectural moldings break up the bold color.

ABOVE: In Palm Beach designer Jennifer Garrigues's living room, pale green walls subtly reflect the tropical landscape. Her collections of art and furniture remind visitors that the exotic outdoors are within easy reach.

On Custom Color

Considering how many sources there are for paints — from Lowe's and Home Depot to paint manufacturers like Benjamin Moore and Pratt and Lambert — it may come as a surprise that so many designers tinker with colors as often as they do or even create custom shades for their clients' homes. "I mix a lot of my colors to get the exact tonality," says Jennifer Garrigues. "Sometimes I'll use a mixture of two or three colors to get something unusual." Designers look for or create colors to match or complement a fabric scheme — if that means creating or tweaking an existing color in order to achieve the desired effect, that's just part of the job. They'll also layer colors to get a desired look, which is what designers Paul Garzotto and the late Marguerite Green did for clients in Dallas. The library was painted in fifteen coats of paint and glaze, which finally yielded the moss green hue they were seeking. "The first coats were chartreuse, and then we applied succeeding darker tones in order to achieve the color," says Garzotto. "That many coats adds richness and depth."

sample swatches:

"*I tend to look at my clients' complexions when I'm working on colors, especially the woman's colorations. I like to use colors that make my clients look good. When I'm at a loss for where to start, I just look out the window. I may see pink, I often see green. It's a very natural way to get started.*" – PHILLIP SIDES

sample swatches:

"These paint colors and fabric swatches work together in a very fluid fashion to re-create the essence of nature through the reflection of color, texture, and light." – JENNIFER GARRIGUES

chapter 3

Reds

Drive through any of the fashionable neighborhoods in the South one evening, and you'll see that window views into the dining rooms reveal rich red walls lit by sconce and candlelight. What is it about the dining experience that has always drawn people to the color red? Perhaps it's the sense of enveloping color and warmth. It's a color thought to stimulate appetites and, hopefully, interesting conversation. It's also undeniably flattering. Think of a brunette or a blonde wearing a red sweater. Skin glows. It's one of those shades that work with all skin types.

Palm Beach designer Jennifer Garrigues says, "Sun colors like red and burnt orange and yellow really work well in dining rooms. They excite the appetite and are romantic and rich. They should stimulate you into a feeling of festivity for feasting." Red bedrooms are another issue altogether. Many designers have done them with both happy and unfortunate results. Garrigues says, "Bedrooms should be calmer, more peaceful. I've done one in red before, but usually I like these rooms to be soothing."

If red stimulates, then orange or pumpkin radiates light. Pink pretties and freshens. The shades are softer, easier on the eyes and the imagination than a bold red, but they are just as engaging when used correctly.

As overall color or an accent, red and its siblings draw the eye and help direct attention around a room or to an object. On paintings and ceramics, pillows and rugs, red provides the punctuation in a well-edited space. As upholstery or wall color, red in a room helps it come alive.

PAGE 74: Painted white and parcel gilt, a pedestal table and frames serve as the backdrop to a collection of vibrant orange and red painted flowers. Though the contrast is stark, it is not off-putting because of the quality of the artwork and the compatibility of the tones.

OPPOSITE: Red Venetian and Bohemian glasses cover a formal tabletop. Their strong tones are mediated by an unexpectedly informal arrangement of purple blossoms and the famille rose finger bowls at each place setting.

OPPOSITE: A coral damask accented with gold thread channels the natural light that pours in the windows of this New Orleans dining room. Red and amber accents abound — in the wood, the pears on the table, even the libations.

BELOW: There is so much available light in this Rehobeth Beach house that Barry Dixon could play with bold, intense shades and create plays of color between all the elements in the room. The white and gilt Regency chairs work with the house's millwork. The red upholstery has a yellow pattern to casually coordinate with the window treatments. The pattern in the window treatments connects to the trim on the chairs. The black basalt urns bring out the touches of black in the window treatments and add a sense of formality to the bright space. Lastly, red and yellow hues are both present in the walnut dining table.

OPPOSITE: A cobalt-glazed Chinese ginger jar, a yellow lamp, and a lot of red — in the books, the art, the rug, the upholstery — all play off one another. The slipcover on the wing chairs — white trimmed in carmine red — brightens the space and reflects the sunlight streaming in the windows.

BELOW: An interesting arrangement, with a console that acts as a sofa table and a gilt, upholstered bench that fills the negative space, gets a jolt of color from the red slipcover.

BELOW: Virginia designer Barry Dixon created a tavern-inspired seating area off to one side of an entry hall. The choice of red upholstery is earthy enough to be consistent with the wood details and stone surfaces but also get attention.

OPPOSITE: Simple red chintz-covered cushions lend color and softness to drawings with their pencil lines faded to gray, as well as wood floors and furniture.

PREVIOUS SPREAD: Deep rust-colored silk window treatments, which act as glamorous extensions of the walls, can be pulled shut to keep light out of the cypress-paneled library. Gold accents in the fabric pick up gold touches in the furniture and carpet.

The "cardinal" sin, painting a bedroom red, is forgiven in a New Orleans *pied à terre*, particularly because French doors let in abundant natural light and the blue window treatments create a surprising but successful contrast. Art brings the red and blue together. On the mahogany bedstead, a red throw and ermine-colored pillow pull out the red accents in the heavily grained wood.

OPPOSITE: Copper pots and red tiles, as well as the terra-cotta tiles on the floor, give a New Orleans kitchen a warm golden cast.

BELOW: Yellow and red seem an unexpected pairing, particularly in a bedroom. But the cozy feeling that red inspires seems sun-kissed in this yellow room.

Red As a Rose

Red is the drama queen of all colors. There is no competing with it, no upstaging it. As an accent or filling a room, it commands all of the attention. It entrances and can be temperamental. It was a dominant color on the walls of Pompeii and Herculaneum, the ancient Roman cities frozen in time by volcanic ash and then excavated in the eighteenth century. Since then, red walls have filled chateaux and palaces across Europe. It's not surprising that the color would also find a place across the Atlantic.

But even before the 1700s, centuries ago in China, craftsmen were making vases decorated with a rich sanguine, or oxblood, glaze. Their elegant shapes as well as the opacity and purity of the color create a striking silhouette in Southern interiors. As vases or turned into lamps, Chinese *sang de boeuf,* or sanguine, vases demand a look and help direct a gaze to its next destination.

For centuries, episcopal and papal robes were rich, carmine red. Today, connoisseurs such as Memphis interior designer William Eubanks collect their magesterial portraits. The dignity of the subjects evokes another time. The painted garments are so intense that they lend authority to any room. The paintings cease to be art for art's sake. The artworks' bold color becomes a component in design schemes. While designers often advise clients to incorporate shots of color into their interiors — in throws, pillows, collections — religious artwork is to be handled delicately. The color clothed reputedly pious people, but it also represented power, sometimes despotic power — not necessarily something you'd want on your walls. But the paintings are beautiful, historical, rich with patina and character — and another way to work color into your home.

OPPOSITE: Subtle touches of red in the sconces and a pale red stripe on the settee and in the area rug give color to the space without overwhelming it.

ABOVE: Bouillotte lamps, originally used in nine-teenth-century France, provided light to those playing bouillotte, a precursor to poker. The lamps were usually lit by candlelight and thus had to have tole shades, which were not flammable. This opaque red shade picks up the red in the wallpaper panel behind it and will direct light downward rather than diffuse it through the room.

TOP, LEFT: A seventeenth-century miniature chair bears its original red velvet upholstery, which gives it a presence much greater than its diminutive size. The diabolical-looking squirrel seems right at home.

BOTTOM, LEFT: Flowers can enhance the colors that you're trying to bring out in an interior. In William Eubanks's house a petite arrangement of red and yellow ranunculus reveals the designer's passion for color.

OPPOSITE: Morning light floods the upstairs stair hall, furnished with a painted and gilded cassone and a comfortable wing chair. "I love wing chairs and French open armchairs," says William Eubanks. "Anything comfortable." The red robes of the Italian cleric inject the space with intense color.

ABOVE: Green accents, in the trellised ceiling, around the chinoiserie panels, on the arched French doors and the upholstery give the airy solarium definition and a distinct relationship with the outdoors. But it's the cherry red wall color that makes the room so stunning and brings out the detail in the panels.

OPPOSITE: Sanguine or red chalk drawings, like these examples from the eighteenth century, are highly sought-after on the art and design market today. The technique captures contours and nuances in the same way blush highlights cheekbones.

We have not seen as many red walls in the past few years in the magazine because of the interest in neutral, calm spaces. But variations on the shade, with a little blue thrown in or softened with white and gray or yellow that inspire a festive, warm feeling are appearing as we are all rediscovering the lasting appeal of color. During the holidays, the classic pairing of red and green is a cliché that never gets old. Since red symbolizes the basic Christian virtues of charity and love and lends color to a season that is otherwise pretty stark, it's a perenially welcome color.

The interiors, no matter the season, that seem the most inspired by tradition, the most adorned with collections, show red to its best advantage. In dining rooms, as well as libraries, living rooms, and even bedrooms, boldly colored red walls and upholstery enhance all the elements of a room — from the bare bones to the accessories. One thing to remember: if red is used liberally, lighting takes on increased importance because red can become very dark if it is not lit adequately.

ABOVE: With early oak paneling, the living room at William Eubanks's home might have seemed very somber. However, the red accents he selected — in the carpets, chintz and red damask upholstery on the Knole sofa, even the paintings — keep the space from feeling heavy. The early-seventeenth-century intricate plaster ceiling covers the room in light. Eubanks loves to mix primary colors in interiors.

OPPOSITE: Deep red velvet and damask upholstery might evoke a Victorian parlor were it not for the austere book spines, antique woods, and blue painted paneling that make the space decidedly, fashionably intellectual.

Orange

At its most vibrant, the color orange conjures up images of the streamlined, modernist furniture of the 1970s, even the hyper chic pieces coming out of Milan today. More subtly, orange evokes the terra-cotta-colored houses of Provence and Mexico, the clay pots that make up the container gardens on our terraces.

Orange appears in the luminescent color field paintings of Mark Rothko, in the opaque tones that fill antique Heriz and Serapi carpets. It has centuries of precedence despite its more recent futuristic incarnations.

Orange occurs in fruit, flora, and fauna, the sunset and the sunrise. It can be surprisingly flattering. Makeup artist Bobbi Brown has based her cosmetics line on the notion that it is a mistake to think that we have pink tones in our complexions. Even the fairest face is shown off to its best advantage with a little yellow and terra-cotta toning.

The color is undeniably stylish. "I love the warmth of pumpkin colors," says designer Barry Dixon. "And chenille and velvet go hand in hand." They're soft and comfortable. In a Rehobeth Beach house, Dixon upholstered several key pieces of furniture with what he calls "pumpkin" to warm up rooms that might otherwise be blown out by the light streaming through floor-to-ceiling windows.

In a way, orange is the sunny offspring of red — strong and intense but full of light. "Strong colors — like orange or red — can be great in a foyer," says Dixon. In the Rehobeth Beach house, he combined the colors in contemporary botanicals by

A chaise longue upholstered in pumpkin and trimmed
in gold reflects colors in the window treatments, the
plaid pillow, and the gazing ball.

artist Matthew Moore and then softened the intensity of the composition with a faux-painted white background. "You don't want a room to be a complete shock, but rather a pleasant surprise," Dixon continues. A choice of orange over red brings a contemporary touch of spirit to a space that might still be filled with antiques and the finest fabrics.

Orange does not have to be called orange. It can be pumpkin or squash, tangerine or apricot. But the thing about orange, much like chartreuse, is that it has to be the right shade. Pumped up to its full strength, it will overpower anything and everything in a room. But mellowed and flavored by its surroundings, it's as vital as red and as enduring as chartreuse. Add a little yellow or white or even pink to soften the jolt that yards of orange fabric or gallons of orange paint might give.

OPPOSITE: Perched on a petite orange painted gueridon table, a collection of red and peach-colored roses heralds timeless and seasonless elegance.

LEFT: Canteloupe-colored walls surround a checkerboard-painted floor and faux leopard print seat cushions in the dining room of Palm Beach designer Jennifer Garrigues. The color combination creates a tension conducive to dining and conversation, while the leopard print is a Garrigues signature, an homage to the exotic.

BELOW: Against a tableau of the purest blue, an outdoor arrangement that includes furniture upholstered in an opaque orange provides a vibrant contrast.

OPPOSITE: The coral Utecht chair was designed by Gerrit Rietveld in the 1930s.

Pink

In the South, pink seems almost synonymous with spring. As azaleas bloom and tulips flower, the landscape — from modest gardens to grand expanses — comes to life. But it isn't just a once-a-year phenomenon. Pink is present year-round, in china that decorates the table, window treatments that frame our windows, and often in rugs that provide the color palette for a room.

A few years ago *Southern Accents* ran a story on Oushak carpets because it seemed that every fine Southern home has one. Woven in Turkey, the pile rugs seem to get more beautiful as they age, their sherbet colors mellowing with the years and exposure to the sun. Even today, as seagrass rugs have become increasingly popular, designers still hunt for an Oushak and use its dominant color — usually a slightly faded rose — to stitch a room's palette together. But there are other rugs — Aubusson, Savonnerie, Agra — and other elements that make pink stand out.

In and outside of the South, people still seem attracted to neutral rooms, but our regional predilection for color has crossed its traditional boundaries. At recent furniture and fabric markets, shades that had not been seen for at least a decade became the breaking news of all the trend-watching reports. Pink is no longer just for a lady's dressing or a little girl's room. Chairs are upholstered in it, prints are accented with it, even candles are colored with the shade that is the most flattering by far.

Hot pink throw pillows add energy to a Charleston entry hall, where soft mocha and natural wood floors set a quiet tone. The pillows soften the space and make it more hospitable, a trait Charleston residents are known for.

Designer Alessandra Branca advises using pink mostly in the bedroom. ("But be sure to include masculine touches for men, otherwise they'll never go for it," she says.) It shows up in living spaces because it makes everyone look good and is so easy to live with. This Palm Beach house may take the idea of living with pink a bit further than the average.

The Palm Beach living room may be painted green,
but the pink accents make it a success. "The home-
owners love color," says Alessandra Branca, "so they
let me play." Inspired by the shades of Palm Beach
clothing icon Lilly Pulitzer, Branca created a palette
that would withstand the test of trends despite its
intensity.

Chicago designer Alessandra Branca designed a home in Palm Beach in the quintessential Lilly Pulitzer pink and green. While the green pervades, it's the pinks in a faux-painted leopard print, in a toile de Jouy, that make the rooms so inviting. "I love the color," says Branca. "And my clients wanted me to really play it up." While the coloration is striking, "the combination is classic," she says. "What could be more Palm Beach?"

In other projects, Branca tends to use pink in bedrooms. "I used a pale blush in one project, a coral in another," she says. "I have to be careful and introduce other colors, so it still feels masculine, less like a boudoir. Men usually fight pink, even though it flatters them too. There has to be a balance."

OPPOSITE: Luxurious silk peach-colored window treatments function as soft counterparts to soaring ceilings expanded by linen white walls. They also mediate the contrast between the painted walls and the natural wood doors.

ABOVE: The grand family room is so large that furniture runs the risk of getting lost. The strong shots of red in the multiple seating arrangements, rug, and window treatments keep the room together visually. Designers Paul Garzotto and the late Marguerite Green pickled the sugar pine in the paneling because regular pine would have been too yellow and distorted the color in the room.

While Branca's Palm Beach project represents a bold use of pink, in other projects and in personal spaces it is insidious — in a good way — inspiring the most demure blushes. She actually has quite a bit of pink in her own living room. Hints of the color accent the room.

Charleston designer Amelia Handegan also seeks out quiet pinks — "I like a very pale pink room" — or vibrant fuchsia to wake up a spot. But she cautions, "Pink is tricky. It gets strong very quickly once applied to walls. A neutralized pink is best — like blush."

In a Charleston house she invigorated the entry hall with two hot pink throw pillows on a neutral settee. The room is mocha, and the hot shot of color brings the area to life. "I prefer not using pastels with pastels. Pink needs more depth in companion colors to look significant," she says. In fact, she would use pink with red, orange, even another shade of pink — "it would rival a well-done white on white room" — before she would put pink with lavender or any other pastel.

On Opening and Closing Space

While architecture can expand or reduce the dimensions of a room literally, color can create the illusion of greater or less space without the hassles of major construction work. "If a living room, dining room, and public rooms are all the same color, then they borrow space from one another," says Bill Ingram. "They appear more open." Painting each room a different color confines them within their architectural boundaries. The color underscores the architectural limits of each room. To create the illusion of a larger room, paint the walls and ceilings the same color. "This camouflages the boundaries in a room," says Dixon.

"If you're in a small room, the color will go denser," says Jennifer Garrigues. "If the room is very big and you don't want it to look so large, go to darker colors. Say you have a den and want it to be cozy — use a rich, not necessarily dark color to make the room very interesting." Paler colors may make a small room appear larger and imply natural light when little exists.

Washington, D.C., designer Victoria Neale created a headboard that is dressed in pink. A pretty paisley provided the romantic inspiration.

Barry Dixon lines lampshades with pink silk so that the light will cast a complimentary glow. He and Jennifer Garrigues each seek out pink light bulbs for the lamps they install in their clients' homes. New Orleans designer Gerrie Bremermann covers furniture with prints that have touches of it. It's a pretty, feminine accent in a space — whether it's the library, the living room, or the kitchen, and both men and women can always benefit from a little tone-enhancing color.

sample swatches:

"Our philosophy has always been that the use of bold color, when tempered by a layering of varied textures and balance of organic and architectural design, creates a timeless expression of refined taste."
— WILLIAM EUBANKS AND PARTNER MITCH BROWN

sample swatches:

"I grew up in Italy, a culture drenched with color, so I'm comfortable with it and I love combining colors that create a tension, an energy — pomegranate rose with chartreuse, puce and eggplant. We see such colors in portraits of the seventeenth century, where color was a sign of wealth and status." — ALESSANDRA BRANCA

chapter 4

Yellows

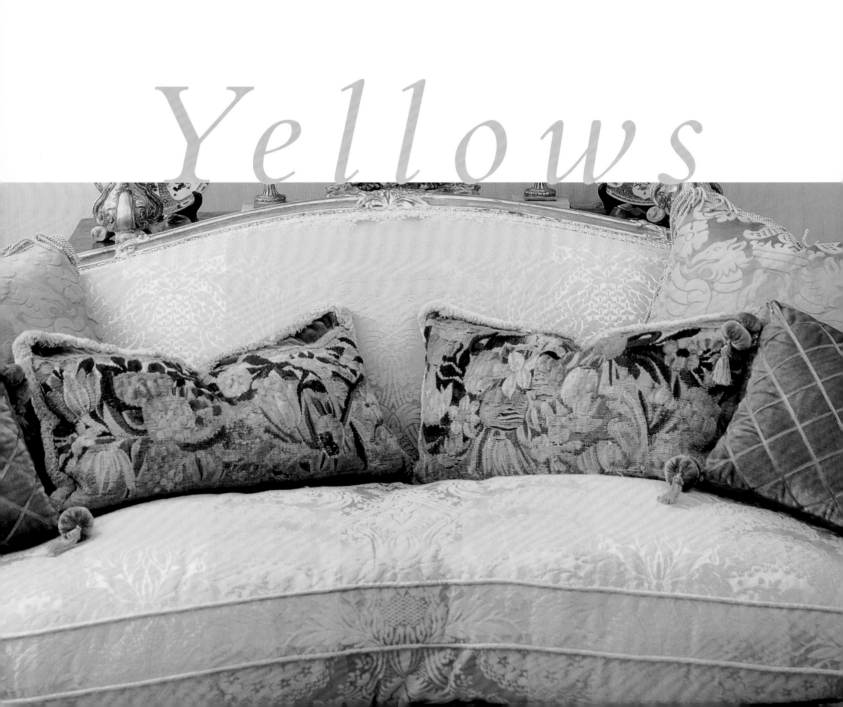

If there is any color that appears most often in *Southern Accents*, it is yellow. Whether soft and buttery, sunny and bold, or golden and radiant, yellow seems to convey a warmth that no other shade can muster. Ever reflective of light, it also brightens dim spaces and gives off an intensity that does not overwhelm. It's also remarkably versatile, functioning often as a neutral. It works well as a backdrop to white, blue, green, gray, brown, purple, and even red, and it can be toned up or down to be as dramatic as Van Gogh's *Starry Night* or as tranquil as Seurat's pointilist works.

In the South, light is traditionally so important and ever present that it makes sense for designers to gravitate toward yellow. Atlanta designer Dan Carithers says, "Yellow will always make a room feel softer." But light also does funny things to yellow, intensifying or dulling it depending on the time of year, the time of day, and the position of the room in relation to the sun. "Yellow will get green if you don't watch it," warns Birmingham designer Phillip Sides.

Yellow's history as a decorative tool is extensive, evident in the ocher colors long associated with Italian and Provencal print designs, as well as the gold in ancient Greece and Egypt. And of course, gold was a precious commodity even in antiquity. But it isn't necessarily yellow's illustrious past that has captured the imagination of so many. What often draws people to yellow is its brightness. "Yellow is a sunny color," says Palm Beach designer Jennifer Garrigues. "It makes people feel good. It's just a happy color — like the sunshine comes out of it."

In accessories and floral arrangements, chromium yellow turns up most often in a brilliant shot that grabs attention and can direct the eye around a room. But it is a bold color, and a little goes a long way. Think of a mass of daffodils or sunflowers — no other flower can compete. Yellow school buses and New York taxis are icons of our contemporary culture. They are unmistakable among the grays of pavement and architecture.

Yellow is as necessary as the sun that inspired it. It is capricious because of its ability to change hues with the subtlest shifts in light, but it can also infuse a space with air and warmth, which is why it has found a welcoming place in Southern interiors.

PAGE 112: A collection of English porcelain depicting scenic landscapes reflects the tone of the walls and the cast of the wood. While the colors don't match perfectly, the yellow is so versatile it enhances the painted scenes on the porcelain.

BELOW: The walls are painted with five coats of high-gloss, thinned oil paint to produce a deep orangey yellow, trimmed in white. Window sashes and doors in the living room and throughout the house are painted in black in classical tradition. Jefferson did it at Monticello, though he used ebony. The effect is to add to the sense of transparency. The panes take on the look of a delicate tracery, not unlike leaded glass.

BELOW: Yellow beadboard walls bring out the yellow in seagrass wall-to-wall carpeting. The spines of the books and the soft pastels in the bed skirt and chair upholstery provide a slight contrast.

OPPOSITE: Yellow is at its best when it is reflecting light. Most often associated with traditional interiors, it finds a place in the seating area of a modern coastal interior, softening the straight lines and bringing in more warmth.

BELOW: Morning light is a wonderful wake-up call, and yellow definitely conveys the feeling. The master bedroom in a Rosemary Beach house, however, is outfitted for those who love the morning but aren't necessarily prepared to greet it first thing. Blackout roman shades and bed curtains in a heavy green print can keep the sun at bay when necessary.

OPPOSITE: The yellow on the chairs and the windows might read as neutral were it not for the weathered gray dining table and the painted breakfront. The waistcoats of the gentlemen in the portraits may have inspired the shade.

Butter Yellow

New Orleans antiques dealer, designer, and historian Patrick Dunne uses a warm yellow in many of his projects. It's the yellow that appears so often in old Provence, sunny and faded under a light that is similar to what we are accustomed to in the South. Faux-painted walls that evoke old stone yellowed by age underscore the sense of age that pervades the Big Easy and Dunne's shops, which feel like very comfortable homes. The yellow is subtle, and the spaces feel hospitable. Antiques, most crafted from French walnut and fruitwoods, fill his shops, casting a warm glow around the spaces. Prints, French genre paintings, and landscapes, as well as centuries-old tapestries, cover the walls. "The strongest element in a house — whether it's a view outside at twilight or a historical watercolor or a piece of furniture — dictates the color you'll use," he says. In Dunne's shops, like the residential projects he designs, the warm patina of antique furniture is the defining element.

In contrast, there are those designers who cover their walls with a yellow that will not settle into the room. Legendary Virginian Nancy Lancaster, who became a celebrated English decorator, transformed design in her adopted country and helped create the English country house look that is widely imitated the world over. She is credited with originating the term "buttah yellah." And the design house that she

RIGHT: Sunlight streams in through the windows and highlights the yellow fabric and paint in fabric designer Grey Watkins's Greensboro, North Carolina, dining room. Even dark touches in the carpet and the mahogany dining table seem brightened by the sunny shade.

OPPOSITE: A collection of blue-and-white porcelain presides over the dining room. The cheery yellow background keeps the room light and not so imposing.

helped build, Colefax & Fowler, maintains that color scheme to this day in the celebrated drawing room of its showroom. The yellow is as fresh now as it was almost a century ago.

One house that borrowed directly from Lancaster's palette has drawing room walls painted in the signature "buttah yellah," and the upholstery complements the shade. Window treatments of striped silk continue the color theme. White painted and black lacquered furniture provides the contrast. A sea grass rug sprawls across the drawing room, allowing the yellow and its counterpoints to stand out. The yellow fills the room and is one step away from dominating it.

Phillip Sides says, "I rarely use a true yellow because I want to relieve the intensity." Instead he "creams it up a bit with brown or red" to relax it. In a house he designed in Birmingham, Alabama, Sides played with the yellows to create transitions from one room to the next. From butter yellows to almost chartreuse, the colors evolve naturally. "Color needs to do what it does," he says, virtually throwing up his hands at the notion that you can control color or manipulate it. "How boring it would be if every color matched all the time. Colors don't match in nature — they should not match perfectly in our houses." It's one thing to say that and another to make it work, but Sides did it in Birmingham. "It gives the rooms a sense of realness to have some shades a little off," Sides says. And they all came together in both the day and evening light. During the day, the walls look almost like ecru linen. At night, under lamplight, they turn a soft shade of yellow as the gold accents and peach-colored fabrics cast a warm glow.

OPPOSITE: Inspired by the renowned yellow drawing room at London's Colefax & Fowler, Dallas designer Cathy Kincaid and British decorator Sarah Morris incorporated an antique tablecloth and traditional fabrics to create a space that reflects the English country look balanced by Southern spirit.

ABOVE: In the dining room of a Birmingham house, designer Phillip Sides went a little darker with the yellow and brought in a light fruitwood as the accent. Gilt accents in the lantern overhead and the lamps on the buffet underscore the gold tones in the room, which only gets more dramatic as the sun descends.

OPPOSITE: In the living room of the same house, Sides played with tones of yellow, some that tended toward apricot, others that wanted to go green. The myriad tones helped them all work together.

Bold Yellow

Memphis designer Bill Eubanks has another take on yellow, in his bedroom of all places. Such a bold color might seem more appropriate to a dynamic space such as an entry hall or a dining room. Eubanks has done something special in recognizing the color he gravitates toward, the shade he wants to surround himself with morning and night. The room radiates sunshine with its bright yellow walls. The inspiration? A bright Oushak carpet. Eubanks incorporates heavy damask and silk fabrics, making this a room not just for the morning sun. Candlelight in the evening provides a romantic flicker of light. And the candles reflect in the extravagantly carved George II–style display mirror that holds part of Eubanks's collection of antique blue-and-white porcelain. "Vibrant yellow light in a room will give the appearance of light even if there isn't actually a lot of natural light in the room," says Eubanks. As it is, the room evokes old England. Its size and architecture recall the grand, drafty castles that dot the English countryside. Warm, heavy fabrics provide sumptuous comfort across the Atlantic. Here in Memphis, the only drafts come from the air conditioning vents in his state-of-the-art home. But Eubanks has re-created the spirit of a place, the romance of architecture, the beauty of tradition. And because it is an English-style estate, where dark wood can make everything seem somber, the contrast of the bold yellow brightens up the space where the designer spends at least eight hours of his day.

An extravagantly carved George II–style display mirror in the bedroom holds part of Eubanks's collection of blue-and-white porcelain. "You can bring in sunlight by painting a golden hue or warm tone on the ceiling," says Eubanks. In his bedroom, the yellow walls bring in sunlight.

LEFT: The shades are so at home with each other that patterns don't compete. In this Rehobeth Beach house, Virginia designer Barry Dixon trimmed the pillow and the curtains in the same pumpkin that appears on the bench upholstery. The paisley throw has both citrine and pumpkin shades, and the trim around the grass carpet also includes both colors.

BELOW: Inspired by the sun rather than the water, Dixon warmed the master bedroom with citrine and pumpkin colors.

OPPOSITE, TOP: A breakfast nook continues the color scheme, where a lighthearted yellow-and-ecru print plays off coral shades on barstools, in pillows, and on the area rug.

OPPOSITE, BOTTOM: The living room in the Rehobeth Beach house is so grand that it might be imposing. Dixon prevented the space from being overwhelmed by filling the room with color and warmth. Yellows and reds all meet in accent pillows, and the cool blue ocean looms beyond, visible through the French doors.

A bright Oushak rug in William Eubanks's master bedroom reflects the sunny color of the walls, citrine yellow softened with an umber glaze. A newly carved giltwood cornice, made by a local Memphis craftsman, tops a Regency bed. The heavy bed hangings are Italian silk damask from Clarence House.

In this Dallas setting, yellow silk upholstery on an
antique sofa and chairs, along with the red wall
color, helps focus the attention where it needs to
go — on the furniture and its lyrical lines. Atlanta
designer Dan Carithers calls chromium yellow
"tense." Here it seems high energy.

Gold leaf has been traced to the tombs of ancient Egypt and the temples of the Aztecs, and it still enthralls. In antique French furniture circles, ormolu-accented objects capture the highest prices at auction. Usually crafted in the finest Parisian ateliers, these pieces of furniture represent the tradition of French cabinetmaking at its best. The quality of the material that went into the construction of each piece was exceptional, and the skill required to work with such precious materials meant that the cabinetmaker, or *ébéniste*, was a master of the art. And it is not just a French tradition. Gilding also occurred in Italy, China, Sweden, and Japan.

Today, those objects are displayed with pride. Contemporary artisans have mastered the old techniques of applying gold leaf with oil (sometimes the oil from the gilder's hair is all that is required), and now walls, ceilings, and other objects are being gilt. Similarly, gold leaf can be restored because the old techniques have not been lost.

The attraction of gilded walls, furniture, and accessories is easy to understand. Gold is, after all, a precious metal. At its worst, it is garish, but in the hands of a talented designer, it does wonderful things with light, reflecting it and helping it move throughout a room. It warms up a space. William Eubanks's marble-tiled entry hall is so grand it risks being imposing, but his addition of stellar 1740 giltwood consoles and antique gilt chairs help warm it. The gold conveys the illusion of light even though there are no windows along the hallway. The space is definitely rich with its great architectural proportions, but the gilded pieces bring another dimension of light into the room.

As much as red — in the portraits and the rugs — has an impact on the room, it is the gold that stands out and gives the room the light it needs to keep from being heavy. The marble-tiled hall runs the length of the house and serves as an informal gallery for William Eubanks's collection of European portraits. The ornate giltwood consoles that flank the gated entryway date from about 1740. Matching blue-and-white jars are early nineteenth century.

Anglophile designer William Eubanks decorated his Memphis home with all the accoutrements of a Jacobean manor. "Because of their rainy days, the English painted their public rooms vibrant reds, blues, yellows, and greens to juxtapose with the gray weather outdoors," he says. His dining room is accented in red, but it is the light yellow on the walls and the rich gold tones of the window treatments that give this room its light and character.

In Eubanks's dining room, a chair covered in velvet embroidered in metallic thread and horsehair is one of the only remnants of the house's original furnishings. The faded patina of the velvet brings out the red tones in the floor and wood frame of the chair, while the yellow window treatments bring out the gold in the metallic thread.

Ocher

Ocher or mustard colors call to mind those pretty printed cotton fabrics of Provence and the olive jars of Tuscany, both with the rich tone of naturally occurring yellow. *Southern Accents* has a certain kinship to these areas, the southern agricultural regions of Europe. France even has its own equivalent magazine, *Coté Sud,* that is as devoted to a regional aesthetic. In this country, there are plenty of houses, many of them new constructions, that strive to recreate the look of Tuscany or Provence with ocher and umber shades. The designers most adept at working with those colors recognize that the light is not quite the same here. Our history is vastly different. A house filled with Provençal fabrics and French farmhouse furniture resembles the fantasy of a contemporary Marie Antoinette, who played peasant on occasion at Versailles. Instead, designers here are reinterpreting the colors of Provence and Tuscany, balancing an appreciation for the spirit and history of Europe with aesthetic traditions that are still shaping the South.

In Dallas, decorator Paul Garzotto painted an entry hall a rich ocher color as a backdrop to two consoles and trumeaux that he had designed. The color enhances the gilding in the furnishings and even brings out the yellow in the paintings at the center of the trumeaux. Texture and depth are implied in the application of multiple layers of paint and glazing. There is no Benjamin Moore reference for this color. Garzotto created it on the walls instead of in a paint can.

A faux painter created pattern on the walls of this Virginia dining room. Yellow that appears on four of the dining chairs and in the window treatments sets the tone for the room. Barry Dixon kept the room from being predictable by upholstering the armchairs in a different complementary fabric that seems inspired by the floor covering.

A similar color in the same house decorates a much less formal space — the upstairs breakfast area. Furnished with antiques as well as comfortable furniture, the room consists of a dense ocher that is made brighter with the addition of pink and yellow chintz upholstery. Red seems a natural counterpoint in the room, but it is the unexpected pink that makes the room feel so vital and animated. The yellow underscores the room's function. Bright and sunny, it prepares the owners for each day's challenges in the most subliminally positive way.

Whether soft or intense, yellow creates a lasting impression. It is an optimistic color, largely immune to trends because of its bright nature.

OPPOSITE: A sunny Dallas breakfast room radiates light from the walls, window treatments, even the flowers. The yellows in the prints and wall color don't match exactly, which gives energy to the space.

ABOVE: Yellow painted and glazed walls in a Dallas hallway bring out the gilding in the consoles and trumeaux — and also serve as a foil to the green library, which also has gold accents.

On Lighting

Your choice of lighting in an interior can affect any color you've chosen for your walls and furniture. It can enliven or drain a person, a mood. The sun's position in relation to a room can alter color, as can the voltage or shade of your light bulbs. There is no more important factor in determining how a wall color or fabric is going to look in a room than light. Before you make any decisions, evaluate your paint and your fabric during the day and at night, as it evolves with the sun and reacts under lamplight. And keep in mind that dark colors absorb light, as does flat paint, while pale colors and gloss paint reflect it. Coastal communities are awash in color. Abundant light keeps colors bright. In contrast, northern areas usually err on the side of softer colors because the light is not as ever present.

Natural Light

Most of us can agree that morning light is pretty wonderful, especially when it streams through undressed windows and bathes everything in warmth. But the sun goes down, and the pace of life requires that we not live, like our forebears did, with the sun's habits. And thank goodness we've progressed beyond firelight, which is lovely on a cold winter evening but hugely impractical in an Alabama August.

Candlelight

Candlelight is the most desirable, if you don't have natural light. "I tell my clients that if they're going to have a dinner party, they should use candlelight," says Jennifer Garrigues. "It really is the most flattering of all lights." Romantic and warm, candlelight evokes the past at any time of year or at any event.

Chandeliers and Sconces

It is still possible to find chandeliers and sconces that have not been altered for electricity, but it is becoming increasingly difficult and not always practical. And there is nothing wrong with chandelier light. "I love tall windows and pools of artificial light — what you get from lamps or fabulous chandeliers," says Patrick Dunne. Sconces in a dining room or hallway also provide enough light to be practical without being shockingly bright. "Beautiful chandeliers should always have a dimmer," says Jennifer Garrigues. "There is nothing worse than overhead lighting that is too bright."

OPPOSITE, LEFT: An avid collector of all things French, New Orleans antiques dealer Kerry Moody painted the walls of his dining room a soft yellow, which comes to life under the glow of candlelight and lamplight.

OPPOSITE, RIGHT: Pale yellow walls provide a neutral backdrop for the boxwood-red apple arrangement and the teal blue tissue paper cones. The lemon tree repeats the yellow.

Recessed Lighting

Overhead lighting is the source of the most consternation among designers. Mindful that it is sometimes a necessity, they are creative in dealing with it. Phillip Sides says, "I learned about recessed lighting the hard way. I kept installing it in my clients' houses, but they never turned the lights on. So now I won't use it unless absolutely necessary." Patrick Dunne simply won't use it. "Americans overlight everything," he says. "Not everything in a room has to be revealed."

The key seems to be in selecting low-voltage lights. "You don't want to highlight everything in a room," says Bill Ingram. "What is dark can be as interesting as what is light. It's good to have a little mystery." Barry Dixon uses incandescent lighting. "It's wonderful in orange-toned rooms," he says.

Lamplight

As an alternative to overhead light, lamplight seems to be the fixture of choice. Dixon and Garrigues both opt for pink light bulbs because they are so flattering. "The Ritz in Paris uses pink lighting, and people wonder why they look so good there," says Jennifer Garrigues. Dixon often lines lampshades in pink silk to ensure a flattering pink glow in a room. One thing to remember is to be careful in selecting your shades. Opaque lampshades will focus light downward, an idea that works particularly well on a desk. Translucent shades help diffuse light throughout the room, a particularly useful tool when you are trying to eliminate the need for recessed lighting.

On Ceilings

When most of us think of color in a room, we look around, at the walls, the upholstery, the floors, the accessories. Who thinks about the ceiling? Designers do. And they all have very definite opinions. Examine the pages of *Southern Accents,* and you'll recognize that you rarely see pure white ceilings or trim. Ceilings and trim are tools that can be colored to add or take away space, to give height or intimacy to a room. They present both an opportunity and a challenge.

"All of my rooms have some kind of color on the ceiling," says Barry Dixon. "There is nothing more awful than a burgundy room with a stark white ceiling," he continues, citing the shock of pairing two diametrically opposed shades. Patrick Dunne says simply, "I don't like white ceilings. I always tint them." At the very least, designers will give the ceiling a hint of color. For example, Gerrie Bremermann takes a portion of the wall color and mixes it with white for a ceiling tint that's lighter than the walls but continues the color.

Birmingham architect Bill Ingram advises using a dark color on the ceiling of a small room. "You would think it closes the room," he says. "But really it expands it, as if the room had more infinity." Color may expand the breadth of a room, but Jennifer Garrigues says it also lowers the ceiling. "If you paint the ceiling a darker color, it will lower it. Alternately, if you paint a ceiling a brighter color, it will raise it," she says. "I usually take a little color that is in the walls and tint it with a creamy white to make the whole room glow."

Dixon uses the same color on the walls and ceiling in a room without crown molding "to tone out the irregularity of the ceiling. If the room is wallpapered, then I wallpaper the ceiling and it has the same effect," he says. "Trim and crown molding break up a room. If you want a bigger room to appear smaller, paint the trim in a crisp contrast. It chops the room up."

Ingram concurs with Dixon about the effects of white crown molding. "Generally I don't like to use white crown molding; it breaks up a room. If it's a flatter paint and not glossy then it looks better. I think that trim and molding need softer finishes."

Of course, some designers and architects are looking back to America's colonial era, when trim, sashes, and doors were painted black. "I think it's interesting to use dark paneled doors," says Ingram. "When doors are painted, they become a more important piece of the room. We love for the door to be different."

sample swatches:

"These are the colors that warm the heart and soul — the sun's helios gamut grounded with earthy clays and burnt oranges — bright in the summer, warm in the winter, they straddle the spectrum between sunlight and candlelight." – BARRY DIXON

chapter 5

Neutrals

esigners whose palettes run more toward the monochromatic always cite a desire for "serenity" as the reason behind the color choice. But as serene an impression a monochromatic room conveys, it is usually far from simple. With layers, textures, and tones, a well-designed monochromatic room may be one of the most challenging to pull off with complete success. All of the variations in color must be complementary, the contrasting textures (i.e., woven, nubby, satiny) not too jarring, and the contrasts themselves — between wood and paint, artificial and natural light, upholstery and details — also complementary.

Because there is so much light in the South and there are so many historical associations with wealth and position in color, the region has been slower to take up the neutral charge. Even in the 1940s, glamorous movies were full of icy blue and white modern lines, while the majestic houses in Nashville's Belle Meade, Houston's River Oaks, and Atlanta's Buckhead were all filled with color.

But with time, attitudes have changed, and some of the South's foremost designers have exploited to advantage the richness of linen white and its ability to reflect the sun that streams in through grand windows. What designers in the South have done is marry the palette of the finest neutrals on the market with the aesthetic that still reigns in the region — good classic design with one foot in the past and one comfortably in the present. There are antiques in the rooms, shots of color from throws and artwork, and contemporary furniture that often embraces a soft palette — a step around neutral. From pure white to ivory, gray, and brown, the South's finest designers have taken a neutral stance that's anything but simple.

PAGE 144: Espresso-colored walls provide a backdrop for antique and new furniture in a Louisiana entry. The wall color almost functions as a picture mat, letting the forms of the furniture and the art stand out. There is so much light coming in through the window, even filtered through the roman shades, that the brown stays brown, not black.

OPPOSITE: A rich tobacco provides the basis for color in the Charleston single house designed by Amelia Handegan. Accents of gold and silver leaf enliven the arrangement in the drawing room. Known for her ability to meld Old World style with contemporary tastes, Handegan used the tobacco color to draw attention to the lines of the antique furniture and original architecture.

Four walls of gray blackout curtains surround a bed and sitting area in Bill Ingram's Birmingham house. The gray serves as a happy medium between the brightness of white — on the bed and furniture upholstery — and the darker brown accents that show up in the mahogany wood.

New Orleans designer Gerrie Bremermann is known for her expert hand with the color white. Bremermann's interiors are all neutrals: crisp white linen, antique lace, vintage chintz that is mellowed to a light pink, and a hint of gold leaf in the art and furniture, such as in an antique Louis XVI chair or an Italian daybed. Her whites are crisp but convey an age, a history. There is something inherently historical in her interiors. The spaces look au courant, but the reference to the past is always there, much like in her native New Orleans.

When many other designers use white, the evocation is of the 1940s and 1950s. The South is not immune to global trends, and there is definite interest at the beginning of the twenty-first century in the fifty years that preceded the turn. Modern furniture designs by Le Corbusier and Mies van der Rohe, upholstered in the palest hues, are appearing as accent pieces in many homes that are featured in *Southern Accents*. From a practical perspective, the prices for less well known designers are not yet outlandish, even though the furniture can be attributed to a specific atelier or designer. Eighteenth-century equivalents regularly break auction records.

Washington, D.C., designer Darryl Carter used white throughout a Palm Beach project that looks modern despite the fact that the furnishings are all antiques and reproductions. Carter might have played off the setting — a condominium in a polo club — and gone for the traditional horsey look of strong plaids and hunter greens. Instead, he sought out antiques and used his own line of reproduction furniture —

Aside from giving a room a sense of calm and a look of pure cleanliness and order, white will make other colors and patterns stand out even more. The damask pattern on the upholstery actually reads in the natural light streaming through windows, and subtle gild-ing contributes to the light reflecting throughout the room. The effect would be diminished with dark floors, which would soak up the natural light reflecting through the room.

OPPOSITE, CLOCKWISE FROM TOP LEFT:
In the tropical climate of Palm Beach, an all-white bedroom evokes an oasis of cool. The large French doors keep the oppressive heat at bay but the lush environment within easy view.

Flokati rugs and modern furniture have made a strong comeback in the last few years, especially as we gain an appreciation for their comfort and simplicity. An all-white background makes the sculptural lines of the leather furniture stand out and the forms on the classic frieze clearly visible.

The only ornamentation in the Memphis guest room designed by Ann Holden of Holden & Dupuy in New Orleans appears on the camel-shaped headboard. Delicate embroidery makes the simple arrangement feminine. The all-white room shifts the focus to the silhouettes rather than a play of colors.

In a Palm Beach living room, designer Darryl Carter selected pieces upholstered in sun-washed whites from his own production furniture line to play off antiques with their mellow patina. The wing chair has very traditional lines, but the clear color makes it feel utterly up to date.

ABOVE: In the heat of a New Orleans summer, dining outdoors is a precious rarity. When the opportunity presents itself, covering a table in a starched white heirloom cloth brings formality outside amid the tropical abundance of the Crescent City.

wing chairs, footstools, French fauteuils, and camelback sofas and settees — and upholstered them all in different shades of white. The home is airy and light, punctuated by dark wood, leather bindings on books, and gilt light fixtures to add some depth. "White needs a tint of warm color to be inviting," says Carter. The patina of the wood, the curves on the furniture, the floor coverings, all contribute to an overall atmosphere that's both cool and calm, as well as invested with style.

Brown

Ten to twenty years ago, working with neutrals meant working with infinite variations of white and ecru. Today, because there is such an increased appreciation for color, neutrals also conjure up images of warm browns and grays. Brown is most often seen in libraries and bedrooms, areas that are associated with intimacy. Its connotations are familiar and friendly — think of a Hershey's chocolate bar. But recently a lighter shade of brown — café au lait or mocha — has appeared in our living spaces. It conveys a richness and sense of history, in much the same way that mahogany or cypress paneling does, but with a softness that comes from the smooth surface of a painted or upholstered wall.

In *Southern Accents,* brown also appears in tailored interiors where wool window treatments, a damask bedcover, or gingham upholstery set the tone. In the Louisiana home of Madeleine Cenac, brown is more incidental but just as powerful. The house, in mid-renovation, is all about brown wood furniture, floors, and exposed brick walls that set the color palette. Anything that contrasts — white muslim, flowers, greenery, a carafe of wine — is just that, a contrast that compels.

But brown is also making forays into untraditional territory, such as the dining room and the kitchen. It's being lightened with yellow or gray, warmed with red. No longer an alternative to black, brown envelops like wood paneling but without the same clubby Edwardian feel.

In the lounge of the Chattanooga house, McAlpine and Booth covered the walls in a brown wool. Accents of gold — the trim around the curtains, the Italian pricket over the mantel, and the studs in the chest and screen — add another dimension to a space that is mostly brown and ivory. The tortoiseshell on the desk may have served as the inspiration for the color scheme.

OPPOSITE: Brown-and-white transferware, like its toile de Jouy cousin, looks particularly good with checks. In this sunny space, Atlanta designer Jackye Lanham matched the background brown to the brown in the collection of plates and then found a plaid that carries the color theme even further. A mahogany hall chair and Pembroke table bring a deeper, redder brown into the arrangement.

ABOVE: In a Virginia master bedroom, Barry Dixon covered most surfaces with a brown-and-white toile de Jouy. A brown plaid custom carpet continues the scheme, but it is the contrasting prints on the chair and ottoman, bed, and pillows that keep it from being overwhelming. The white upholstery and white painted chest give the room a sense of openness. Notice the brown border in all the bed and window treatments, underscoring the room's consistent color scheme.

RIGHT: In Chattanooga, dark wood flooring creates a provocative contrast with white walls in the entry hall of an antiques-filled house. The deep charcoal stools offer unobtrusive seating.

But, of course, a little goes a long way. A room weighed down by too much English mahogany or French walnut runs the risk of being somber. Similarly, a house covered room by room in brown evokes a time before any color choices existed — and not in a good, romantic way. In a Virginia house, Barry Dixon played with brown in all the rooms, but he was constantly keeping things from getting too somber by injecting color — yellow, red, black, pink — to keep things interesting.

At *Southern Accents,* we love antiques, but too many stories on brown furniture and neutral interiors tend to leave readers unsatisfied, longing for color. We look for a balance between brown's stable character and color accessories that add a lighter feel and give each issue a personality that's as light and fun as it is informative.

The scale and design of the house evoke the Middle Ages interpreted with an eye to Arts and Crafts, so designer Barry Dixon took his cues from the aesthetics of the eras, always keeping in mind today's very contemporary interest in comfort. The four chairs in the largely neutral music room are covered in a black silk and wool bouclé embroidered with copper and silver threads. Black typically might seem heavy, but the large scale of the room and the softness in the background make the chair fabric a compelling choice.

OPPOSITE, RIGHT:

Designers often refrain from coloring libraries so that the color of the books' spines provides the palette. In this room, paneling cut from dead standing oak trees in Pennsylvania reach ten feet toward the soaring ceilings. Framed prints fill the space between the paneling and the ceiling.

BELOW, LEFT:

Prints commissioned by Sir William Hamilton after the discoveries of Pompeii and Herculaneum in the eighteenth century cover tobacco-and-gold-striped wallpaper in the small dining room of a Dallas house. Embroidered linen slipcovers feature prints that are subtle enough not to compete with the art.

BELOW, RIGHT:

Originating in the sixteenth century in Europe, barley twist furniture has been revived throughout history. Now we seek pieces not only for their sculptural quality but also for the dark brown patina of the wood. The armchairs are circa 1820 France; the candlestick table is circa 1880 England.

ABOVE: Wall-to-wall seagrass provides a neutral backdrop on floors and an easy way to bring a very formal space a bit more down to earth. It works particularly well as a counterpoint to the very sculptural wood elements — the reproduction Regency table, the Regency chairs, the cabinet, even the silk draperies — in a Birmingham dining room. The pretty porcelain adds a nice touch of pattern.

RIGHT: The mahogany-paneled library cloaks the room in a warm glow, where leather and velvet make welcoming props.

OPPOSITE: A traditional dining room, with damask-covered walls, Regency chairs, and a large round table at its center, does not have the traditional coloration of red or yellow. Instead brown, gray, and black set a quiet tone, letting floral arrangements, colorful china, and food take center stage.

Brown is the color of choice in Madeleine Cenec's Louisiana drawing room because the exposed brick and wood beams dictate the palette. Still, more formal French antiques seem at home in the setting, not because of their compatible colors but of their sympathetic spirits. The color on the door, Prussian blue, was chosen based on traces of paint found throughout the Creole house.

Zen simplicity, free of the clutter and collections that
stir memories good and bad, relies on natural materials. In this Houston home, luxurious fabrics cover
furniture with strong silhouettes. The art came from
writer Carol Barden's travels to the Far East, as did
the aesthetic inspiration.

Silver and Gray

While stark all-over black and white are greeted mostly with a wince when it comes to interiors, there is something very comforting about the meeting of the two in the form of gray. Ironically, black — every woman's uniform at the turn of this century — turns a home into a haunted house. Its lighter counterpart seems much more hospitable. Similarly, flat white, so lovely in linen on a summer day and so beautiful draped across a table, can seem ultramodern and harsh when it covers walls and ceilings. But gray, like a tailored flannel suit, takes away all sharp edges, all harsh glares, and appears infinitely livable.

What makes it so appealing is its kinship to other frequently used shades. Gray might have a touch of blue that makes it icy; silver, giving it a flash of luxury; or yellow for a bit of warmth.

In the South, silver inherited, registered for, collected over the years takes up some part of every household. It may be stored away in felt bags to fend off tarnishing oxi-

OPPOSITE: In a dining room that evokes the interiors of the late Elsie de Wolfe more than the tony neighborhood of Highland Park in Dallas, silver-leaf paper, gray silk window treatments, and painted Chippendale-style chairs combine in a setting that is layered in elegance.

LEFT: A silver wine cooler transforms coxcomb massed into a ball. The simple flower becomes an elegant extension of the silver sculpture and creates a bold contrast that enlivens the Dallas dining room.

BELOW: An old church marquee, retrofitted with silvered glass, hangs over an antique yew wood chest in an entry. The elements of this Chattanooga room are all old, but the absence of saturated color makes the space seem modern.

OPPOSITE: Birmingham architect Bill Ingram credits his pet weimarainer as inspiration for the neutral palette that runs through his house. Pecky cypress paneling and a soft gray-green on the walls reflect the tones in the silk damask on the Saladino slipper chairs and the antique painted chest.

LEFT: Mineral colors abound in the Chattanooga salon, where an antique fall-front desk is topped by an upholstered cabinet. The plainness of the neutral upholstery and sisal rug is broken up by the iron table and Regency-style chair.

BELOW: The Chattanooga sun porch, furnished with a custom chaise upholstered in outdoor fabric, is surrounded by windows providing infinite views of the area. The abundant light will mellow the gray fabric even more over time.

dation or displayed atop the sideboard and polished weekly by some diligent soul. At *Southern Accents,* we've discovered an appreciation for the look of slightly tarnished silver and its coppery glow, an implied patina that takes months rather than decades or centuries to accumulate.

No matter the style, be it modern or traditional, full of color or neutrals, Southern interiors have some silver in them. As objects to collect, silver pieces suggest taste and sophistication. And it may be the only collectible metallic that actually engenders a feeling of warmth, not because of its appearance but because of everything silver connotes — history, hospitality, style. Displayed individually on a tabletop, such as a sideboard, side table, or dining table, or massed in a bookshelf, silver reflects color and light and enhances whatever shade it neighbors.

As silver's sedate cousin, gray has become an element of virtually every color discussed thus far. Designers that tend toward the minimalist say they like gray-greens, blue-grays, gray with some red in it. The gray tones down the colors, making them softer, almost more aged in appearance. With the current emphasis on natural materials — making up walls and floors, counter and tabletops — it seems only natural that gray would find space in today's interiors. Limestone and poured concrete floors, while decidedly hard and not prone to the same creaks and warps as wood, also seem part of the earth and can do a lot to communicate that ever-desired idea of connecting the outdoors to the in.

A house Nashville architect Bobby McAlpine and designer Ray Booth worked on in Chattanooga is filled with what the team calls "mineral colors" that let in abundant light and stand in quiet contrast to occasional punches of color in pillows, paintings, and greenery from the mountaintop landscape. Antique mirrors made from silvered glass set a cool tone in the salon, and the feeling continues to the sun porch, where a granite-topped table coordinates with the gray outdoor fabric upholstery. Despite the fairly monochromatic scheme, the house is layered in color — brown mahogany and

walnut wood, the gray upholstery, the silvered mirrors, shots of color in art and throws that bring out lines in the furniture, fabric, and wall color.

The owners joke that guests have a hard time deciding whether to call the house classic or modern — classic because the house combines traditional antiques and clean lines, modern because the palette is so subtle, so spare, the lines so straight and without fuss, that this house could be a penthouse in New York — were it not for the lush landscape visible through the windows. The debate reflects the versatility of the gray that serves as the dominant color. After all, the house is one hundred years old and

OPPOSITE: A limestone floor in the sunroom of a Greensboro, North Carolina, house provides a natural transition to the outdoors. The striped upholstery on the iron furniture is a livelier alternative to the ubiquitous ecru that covers most outdoor chairs.

ABOVE: For the Chattanooga kitchen, in contrast to kitchens that are colored from top to bottom, perhaps in an attempt to mimic the colors of the food on display, Nashville designer Ray Booth and architect Bobby McAlpine opted for a sedate space where the natural colors of fruit and vegetables will stand out rather than blend in.

BELOW: Filled with sunlight, the interiors of this Seaside, Florida, house have an ethereal feel. The black ash dining table and chairs bring the room back to earth.

OPPOSITE: Black striped curtains pick up the accents of black throughout the room — in the fireplace surround, the black lacquer cabinet, the art. The room is full of antiques and art, but the curtains and their bold stripes give it a contemporary feel.

filled with antiques, two very important elements that make up a traditional interior. But the cool palette lets the identity of the owners and their preferences show through, and the result is a classic modern interior, one that transcends dating.

Black may be the most somber color in existence, but it also can create definition, provide an anchor, lend a striking contrast. And while some may say that they would never live with black, it has a way of showing up in even the most traditional spaces. Charcoal drawings, executed by history's great artists for centuries, are widely collected these days. Toile de Jouy in black and white reappears often in the pages of *Southern Accents*. Black lacquer coffee and side tables have taken up residence in contemporary interiors because of their elegance, simplicity, and unobtrusiveness in an interior. Even wrought-iron furniture, once relegated to porches and patios, is coming indoors as bed frames, coffee tables, kitchen chairs. While the idea of covering a wall with black seems an impossibility, the reality of using accents of the color to help direct the eye around a room, to provide interest, has been happening as long as we've been decorating our houses.

On Art

Too often when considering art and color, the process becomes intimidating or we take the easy way out and try to match a color in a painting with the color for the wall and fabrics. This does a disservice to the art and to us.

Buy art that you love. You'll be surprised how well it will work in your home — if you also love your home.

"If someone has a serious art collection," says Barry Dixon, "I don't use strong color in the room. It's important that the strongest element be the art."

A collection with a lot of bright, vibrant colors can take on an equally vibrant color on the walls behind, advises Dixon. "But the art and wall colors do not have to match. You must consider the art first."

"Painters did not paint their works so that someone would put a spotlight on them," says Phillip Sides. Not all paintings require spotlights. "Leave a little mystery," he says.

If you're hanging a related collection of prints or drawings, consider the wall's color as a mat that will pull all of the individual works together.

Selections of frames and mats should work both with the art and the walls behind them. Black or dark wood frames draw attention. Silver or neutral frames are subtle, sort of standing back to let the art itself take center stage and making it easier to consider a series of works as a whole.

sample swatches:

"*I'm drawn to neutrals, to restful colors. With neutrals, there is always a color that comes through. Most people think of white or off-white, but I see greens that convey calm and give depth to a room.*" – BILL INGRAM

RESOURCES

Fabric Manufacturers

Beacon Hill
(212) 421-1200

Bennison
(212) 223-0373

Bergamo
(212) 888-3333

Boussac Fadini
(866) 268-7722 toll-free

Brunschwig & Fils
(212) 838-7878

Carleton V
(718) 706-7780

Christopher Norman
(212) 647-0303

Claremont
(212) 486-1252

Clarence House
(212) 752-2890

Colefax & Fowler
(England)
44-207-493-2231

Cowtan & Tout
(212) 753-4488

Creation Baumann
(516) 764-7431

Decorators Walk
(212) 415-3955

Dedar
(800) 493-2209 toll-free

Designers Guild
(England)
44-207-243-7300

Donghia
(800) 366-4442 toll-free

Fortuny
(212) 753-7153

Henry Calvin
(888) 732-1996 toll-free

J. Robert Scott
(212) 755-4910

Jim Thompson
(800) 262-0336 toll-free

Kravet
(212) 421-6363

Larsen
(212) 647-6900

Lee Jofa
(888) 533-5632 toll-free

Manuel Canovas Inc.
(212) 997-7411

Nobilis
(800) 464-6670 toll-free

Old World Weavers
(212) 752-9000

Osborne & Little
(212) 751-3333

Pierre Frey
(212) 213-3099

Quadrille
(212) 753-2995

Raoul Textiles
(805) 965-1694

Rodolph
(707) 935-0316

Rogers & Goffigon, Ltd.
(212) 888-3242

Rose Cumming
(212) 758-0844

Scalamandre
(212) 980-3888

F. Schumacher & Co.
(212) 415-3900

Stroheim & Romann
(718) 706-7000

Thibault
(212) 355-5211

Travers
(212) 888-7900

Zimmer + Rohde
(212) 758-5357

Paint Manufacturers

Benjamin Moore
www.benjaminmoore.com

Donald Kaufman Color Collection
www.donaldkaufmancolor.com

Farrow & Ball
www.farrow-ball.com
(845) 369-4912

Martha Stewart Everyday Colors
www.marthastewart.com

Martin Senour
www.martinsenour.com

Pratt & Lambert
www.prattandlambert.com
1-800-BUY-PRATT

Sherwin-Williams
www.sherwin-williams.com

Silk Dynasty Inc.
(877) 734-9255 toll-free

Designers

Alessandra Branca
1325 North State Parkway
Chicago, IL 60610
(312) 787-6123

Gerrie Bremermann
3943 Magazine Street
New Orleans, LA 70115
(504) 891-7763

Lars Bolander
240 Worth Avenue
Palm Beach, FL 33480
(561) 832-5108

Dan Carithers
2300 Peachtree Road, NW
Suite B-102
Atlanta, GA 30309
(404) 355-8661

Barry Dixon
Barry Dixon, Inc.
8394 Elway Lane
Warrenton, VA 20186
(540) 341-8501

Patrick Dunne
Lucullus
610 Chartres Street
New Orleans, LA 70130
(504) 528-9620
lucullus@bellsouth.net

William R. Eubanks
William R. Eubanks Interior
1516 Union Avenue
Memphis, TN 38104
(901) 272-1825
www.williamreubanks.com

Jennifer Garrigues
308 Peruvian Avenue
Palm Beach, FL 33480
(561) 659-7085
www.jennifergarrigues.com

Paul Garzotto
4445 Travis Street, Suite 101
Dallas, TX 75205
www.greengarzotto.com

Amelia Handegan
Amelia T. Handegan, Inc.
165-A King Street
Charleston, SC 29401
(843) 722-9373

Holden & Dupuy
3240 Magazine Street
New Orleans, LA 70115
(504) 897-1100

Bill Ingram
2205 7th Avenue South
Birmingham, AL 35233
(205) 324-5599

Jacquelynne P. Lanham
472 East Paces Ferry Road
Atlanta, GA 30305
(404) 237-8606

Bobby McAlpine
McAlpine, Booth and Ferrier
Interiors
112 Second Avenue North,
Suite 301
Nashville, TN 37201
(615) 259-1222

Phillip Sides
3017 Second Avenue South
Birmingham, AL 35233
(205) 328-6106

Precious Commodities
From The World of Gemstones,
www.gemstone.org
Red: Ruby, garnet
Pink: Ruby, sapphire, topaz, tourmaline
Orange: Sapphire, garnet, mandarin garnet, citrine, topaz, fire opal
Gold: Sapphire, citrine, topaz, amber, tourmaline, garnet
Green: Emerald, tourmaline, peridot, jade, sapphire
Blue: Sapphire, aquamarine, topaz, tourmaline, lapis lazuli, turquoise
Violet: Amethyst, garnet, sapphire, tanzanite, jadeite
Multicolor: Ametrine, opal, tourmaline

What Colors Suggest
Pink: Sweet and affectionate
Yellow: Energetic and warm
White: Pure, clean, and energetic. It makes other colors stand out.

Brown: Earthy and stable
Orange: Cheerful, stimulating, and bold
Red: Dramatic, passionate, stimulating
Green: Calm, stable, vibrant, a new neutral
Purple: Mysterious, regal, spiritual
Blue: Pure, cool, peaceful

Floral Shades
Blue: Muscaris, hydrangeas, bluebells
Purple: Iris, violets, lilacs, tulips
Red: Roses, amaryllis, tulips, anemones, poppies
Orange: Black-eyed Susans, birds-of-paradise
Pink: Roses, hydrangeas, carnations, peonies, tulips
Yellow: Daffodils, sunflowers, roses
Green: Bells of Ireland
White: Roses, carnations, oak leaf hydrangeas, calla lilies, lilies of the valley, lilies, daisies, peonies
Brown: Stephanotis

Fabric Swatch Credits

Page 36 (Jacquelynne P. Lanham)
Top, left to right: Chittagong by Osborne & Little, source not available, Coconut Grove by Schumacher
Middle, left to right: Fulham Linen Velvet by Lee Jofa, Dampierre by Quadrille, Westminster by Lee Jofa, Antico Damask by Schumacher
Third row, left to right: source not available, source not available, Orient Camel Hair (seagrass rug) by Eve Smith Co.
Bottom, left to right: Deep Bronze, Wythe Blue, Moonlight White, all by Benjamin Moore

Page 37 (Gerrie Bremermann)
Top, left to right: Sikandra by Zimmer + Rohde, Shaker by Rogers & Goffigan, Richelieu by Fortuny
Middle, left to right: Ultra 155 by Creation Baumann, P32853 by Peter Schneider (discontinued), Satin La Tour by Brunschwig & Fils
Bottom, left to right: 1095, Bone White, White Dove, 956, White Coffee, Decorator's White, 957, all by Benjamin Moore

Page 72 (Phillip Sides)
Top, left to right: Gran Raya Mandarin Woven, Isla Marada Cotton Print, and Astorga Woven, all by Brunschwig & Fils
Bottom, left to right: Yorke Chenille and Gaston y Daniela, both by Brunschwig & Fils

Page 73 (Jennifer Garrigues)
Top, left to right: Bananier by Boussac, Eden by Raoul Textiles, Spinnaker by Osborne & Little, source not available
Middle, left to right: Marzipan, Hellebore, and New Bamboo, all by Martha Stewart Everyday Colors
Bottom, left to right: Gouache by Designers Guild through Osborne & Little, Verel de Belval by Brunschwig & Fils, Mistral by Designers Guild through Osborne & Little

Page 110 (William R. Eubanks)
Top, left to right: Velvet Ribbon by Decorator's Walk, Fayence by Pierre Frey, Peony by Old World Weavers
Second row, left to right: Bacchus by Scalamandre, Reine Victoria by Clarence House, Brisaac by Old World Weavers
Third row, left to right: Hand Glazed Wall Finish in Cinnabar by Silk Dynasty Inc., Richelieu by Fortuny, Vivaldi by Fortuny, source not available
Bottom: source not available

Page 111 (Alessandra Branca)
Top, left to right: Chinese Pheasant on Silk by Bennison, source not available, Palma Damask by Claremont
Middle, left to right: Bently by Travers, Claremont
Bottom, left to right: Lafayette by Charles Berger, Silk Stripe by Rose Cumming Chintzes, source not available

Page 143 (Barry Dixon):
Top, left to right: Galliera by Boussac, Trinidad by Scalamandre, Rainbow Check by Cowtan & Tout, Lutèce by Pierre Frey
Second row, left to right: Amalfi Velvet by G. P. & J. Baker at Lee Jofa, Porticcio by Pierre Frey, Lama by Boussac, Oudapoor Paisley by Quadrille
Third row, left to right: Braquènie and Lie by Pierre Frey; Surat, Vendôme, and Petit Carrousel, all by Nobilis
Bottom row, left to right: Leaf Scroll by Hodsoll McKenzie, Burdal Wils by Osborne & Little

Page 175 (Bill Ingram)
Top, left to right: Canon Check Summer by J. Robert Scott, Illusion by Larsen
Middle, left to right: Intuition by Larsen, Sugar Cane by Larsen
Bottom, left to right: Kings Ransom by Rodolph, Silk Tapis by J. Robert Scott, Davy's Grey and Light Olive, both by Pratt and Lambert

Photography Credits

Antoine Bootz
v, 60, 75, 85, 86, 87, 95, 141, 150, 153

Monica Buck
7

Cheryl Dalton
115

Pieter Estersohn
ii, xi, 4, 5, 6, 19, 20, 24, 25, 28, 29, 30, 33, 35, 38, 41, 42, 46, 53, 56 bottom, 57, 60, 62, 70, 77, 80, 81, 82, 83, 90 top left, 92, 99, 103, 107, 131, 137, 138, 139, 147, 148, 149, 156 top, 158, 159 left, 160 top, 164, 165, 167

Tria Giovan
viii, xii, 22, 23, 44, 47, 48, 50, 51, 61, 63, 65, 66, 67, 68, 69, 71, 74, 79, 84, 89, 96, 100, 109, 116, 118, 119, 120, 124, 125, 128, 129, 163, 170

Thibault Jeanson
v, 43, 49, 55, 56 top, 58, 78, 90 bottom, 91, 94, 104, 105, 113, 127, 130, 132, 134, 135, 144, 162, 173

Jeff McNamara
101, 117, 172

Howard L. Puckett
90 top right

Andreas von Einsiedel
112, 121, 122, 160 bottom

William Waldron
iv, v, xiv, 1, 3, 8, 10, 11, 12, 13, 14, 16, 17, 26, 95, 106, 145, 150, 152, 155, 156 bottom, 157, 161, 166, 168, 171

Charles E. Walton IV
iv, 39, 54, 159 right

Ka Yeung
98